BIKEPACKING

→

Exploring the Roads Less Cycled

gestalten

CONTENTS

SLOW IS OK

→

FOREWORD
STEFAN AMATO

THE TERM "unhurried" is well-known in the spirit world, to amplify an ageing process that cannot be forced or sped up. And why should it be? Slow is worth the wait; slow is special. Yet, it is only the recent years of adventuring by bike, that I've realized the unhurried nature of bikepacking—experiencing and going places, but without much urgency of arrival—is what really makes our pursuit. On a bike there is only so much ground you can cover, only so fast you can ride, and in this current age of "instant", adventuring into the unknown on a loaded bike with everything you could need is just the tonic.

Strapping kit to bikes is nothing new, of course—intrepid folk have been traveling since the earliest bikes were available in the late 1800s. The first known "celebrity" bike traveler was documented as Thomas Stevens, who set off from San Francisco on his precarious high-wheeler in 1884 and rode (/pushed) across the USA, continental Europe, and Southeast Asia to Japan. Bikepacking is a fresh term, widely regarded as the minimalist, off-the-beaten-track evolution of traditional bike touring—a fusion of multiday backpacking and mountain biking that enables the ultimate freedom: "fast enough to cover a whole continent in a reasonable time but slow enough to see very many interesting things," as experienced traveler Frank van Rijn says best. Bikepacking, as a pursuit, has been made more accessible by the recent emergence and specialization of machines ("all-road" bikes) and

tools (lightweight bags and camping/cooking kit). With the Bikepacker Setup on page 12, for example, cyclists can continue where established roads or tracks end, and, with a bit of effort, can link up the remotest of routes previously reserved for backpackers.

This book is designed to celebrate this life in the slow, off-the-beaten lane—active travel and the sense of adventure, independence and the freedom at bikepacking's core. Over the next pages, you'll find yourself immersed among a host of geographies and terrains—from overnight city escapes in Europe to two-week expeditions in the Tibetan backcountry. But, if there was one recurring theme riding through it? Bikepacking is not all about the bike, more the journeys and worlds it opens up: remote mountain passes and hidden suburbs; alpine hut arrivals and lowland bivvy lookouts; coastline crab cookouts and col-top coffee stops; plunge-pool swims and shoreline surf spots; group social and solo challenges; tame tarmac and gnarly gravel; challenges and cultures; and, most of all, people, place, and possibility.

The last pandemic months have made armchair travelers of all of us—collating this book has fueled my wanderlust no end, as I hope it does for you, for when our playgrounds slowly open up again. All the wonderful contributors are people I've either ridden with, or those that inspire me and I've admired from afar. The book invites you to read about their journeys, from beginner

to expert, short to long, mild to wild, solo to family trips with young children. Their variety means you're pretty much guaranteed to find an inspiring route that you could embark on yourself—after all, bikepacking doesn't have to mean long haul, original, or groundbreaking. If the pandemic has shown us anything, it is an appreciation for local, accessible adventures and escapes from your doorstep, and the importance of stewardship of the great outdoors and the world's wild places.

Through the last decade that I've been involved in the bikepacking scene, I've seen the growth in popularity of escaping by bike, and in particular taking the tracks less traveled. I've seen modest makers thrive, and the mass market seep in: bag makers to bike builders, to clothing and snack makers, and a surge in events and experiences. Grassroots bikepack racing is also caught in a tailwind of popularity—as an amateur, you could find yourself lining up against professional road cyclists keen for something different, a new challenge, an escape. It's been a great journey, and I'm looking forward to seeing where we end up. All I know is, the more people heading further and farther on bikes, the better. This book is meant simply as a start, a spark. So, whether experienced bikepacker or new to the pursuit, I hope this book and its terraneous tales open up a whole new exciting world of possibility. An unhurried world, of course.

See you out there… ○

STEF

HOW TO PLAN A ROUTE

The nature of multiday journeys off the beaten track means some basics need planning. With rugged terrain more of an attraction than an obstacle for bikepackers, route planning—the finest armchair going—is about unlocking the finest places to ride and reach by bike, and seeking and connecting outlying points of interest with the best roads, tracks, and trails…

TRIP PLANNING CHECKLIST

- *Solo or squad—abilities and objectives*
- *Length—time and distance*
- *Route inspiration—ideas, places, and established routes*
- *Research—seasons/climates, history, gastronomy, and wildlife*
- *Start/end points—point-to-point or circular?*
- *Transport options*
- *Terrain—rough roads, technical singletrack, tarmac, and hike-a-bike*
- *Cultural/interest route points*
- *Challenge route points*
- *Stages—daily distances, elevation, and overnight options*
- *Food/water resupply options*
- *Backup route options*
- *Route finalization*
- *Weather check—day/night temperatures and trail conditions*
- *Bike, bags, and kit list*
- *Navigation*
- *Language*
- *Currencies*
- *Permits/visas/vaccinations*

ROUTE INSPIRATION

Throughout the book you will see bike journeys inspired by alluring photos, gastronomy, people and history, challenges, conservation, a lust for discovering new places, or a simple desire to escape the city for a night or weekend. Starting out? Go for a simple S24O (sub 24-hour overnighter) adventure. Take a train somewhere and ride home, or link up two cities or towns you know with as much off-road riding as possible. Partnering up with someone who has bikepacked before or joining an organized bikepacking trip are great for gaining confidence and experience.

Starting from scratch? The possibilities are endless, but even the most established bikepacking routes start with a basic idea. Mac McCoy regales the first conversation about trailblazing the Great Divide Trail in 1990: "Let's map a mountain-bike route along the Continental Divide from Canada to Mexico, remaining as close to the geographical line as possible, while following dirt and gravel roads, and passing through a reasonable number of resupply towns." In a similar geographical-inspired vein, the Torino-Nice Rally route emerged from James Olsen's passion for mapping, seeking, and riding big open alpine tracks. "The Strada dell'Assietta—a 34-kilometer (25-mile) dirt road on the shoulder of a 2,000-meter-high (6,560-foot) mountain ridge—always stood out to me," says James. The route ended up forging the main spine for his 700-kilometer (435-mile) route to the south coast. Alan Goldsmith's Highland Trail endeavor originated from a "need for a tough training route to prepare for the Colorado Trail Race," and at the other end of the spectrum, Stefan Amato mimicked a scene in the film *Trainspotting* for a three-day Pannier.cc trip in the Grampian Mountains: "Alighting the sleeper train at the highest, remotest station in Scotland before connecting up established gravel routes, unknown hike-a-bikes across infamous moors, ace places to stay, and a whisky distillery."

Others, like Ernesto Pastor in Spain, understand the power that bikepacking has to highlight rural or conservation issues. "Routes need a story behind them. I want bikepackers to feel the emptiness and solitude they crave, but also witness the social and geopolitical pressures this has on the stunning, yet depopulated, Spanish Lapland region between Madrid and Valencia," says Ernesto.

ROUTE MAKING

A typical day's bikepacking looks something like 50–150 kilometers (30–90 miles), with 500–2,000 meters (1,640–6,562 feet) climbing. Riding loaded bikes off-road means a pace of 15 kph (3–9 mph), depending on terrain and pauses for food, or unexpected wild swims.

To get the detail required for planning off-road bikepacking routes, you need a map at a scale of 1:50,000 or less. Digital maps are great, but it's hard to disagree with Stuart Wright of Bear Bones' view that "paper maps give a far better overview than you ever can get on a screen. It's easier to see the 'bigger picture' and all available options. Open any map and there'll be hundreds of routes staring back at you; the skill lies in being able to see them." Look for the alluring dashed-lines and smallest roads—less established on the map, less established on the ground—which usually make for the finest terrain. Do your best to check they're safe (and legal) to ride. Alan spent "hours each winter marking up maps with a highlighter pen" to refine the current Highland Trail route. In Scotland "double-dashed lines on maps mean fast/easy going off-road; single-dashed lines could mean anything from sublime singletrack to a route that is non-existent on the ground. The fun is in finding out what is out there." In a similar way, James roughed out his Torino-Nice Route by "plotting Google Earth pins on high dirt roads or places that looked worth exploring" before linking them up with dramatic roads through the mountains. Once you →

have studied the possible paths, begin to plot a route on GPX software while visualizing how to stage the trip, taking into account distances, overnights, and resupply. Platforms like Strava, Komoot, Ride With GPS, Maps.Me, and Gaia GPS, with offline compatibility, enable you to look for tracks less traveled, and check gradients and overall height gains before heading out. Additional tools like Google Street View or Strava Global Heatmaps can be useful for knowing what a particular section might look like or how popular it is. However, James offers caution: "There's a fine line in the detail I want to know beforehand, at the risk of lessening the sense of adventure when actually out riding."

Backup and bailout route options are always a good idea when heading into the backcountry. As Alan says, "I think my gamble of including hike-a-bike sections pays off as riders are excited to get into spectacular and remote areas, but the route's deliberate three loops enable two obvious opportunities to cut the ride short if needed."

NAVIGATION
A highlighted map is arguably the most dependable but stop-start method of navigating on the move. Smartphones with a navigational app with an offline mode and a solid mount do everything you need for finding your way, but a dedicated GPS device like a Garmin or Wahoo are best for following a bikepacking route, not least for

managing a charge, and your cockpit feng shui. Still, Stefan is careful to add that "GPS and the relative simplicity of following a route line have changed the way we navigate and know the outdoors, so be prepared for digital glitches, failure, and needing to edit things. Knowing where you are riding and carrying back-up route-maps/notes is good practice."

Keeping electronics charged on a trip is best with a USB battery pack (10,000 mAh or more). For longer trips off the beaten track, look into a dynamo hub that enables a self-sufficient way of charging via USB, and can also solve your lighting issues. Try not to allow electronics to get too cold or the power will drain. Take them into your tent or sleeping bag overnight. ○

BIKES, BAGS, & SETUPS

Ride. Drink. Eat. Sleep. Repeat. For wilderness wanderers, the development of rackless bags, lightweight technical kit, and "all-terrain" bikes means that all the gear you need can be carried nimbly. Bike and setup versatility—the ability to both pedal off-road passes and comfortably cruise sealed roads—is key for bikepacking trips. Adapt your plans to the bike and kit you have.

BIKEPACKING BAGS

Total capacity will be based on bike size and space available. Always measure and check with bag manufacturers.

1 *Seat pack (8–16 L)*
2 *Handlebar pack (8–18 L)*
3 *Handlebar pouch pack (1–3 L)*
4 *Frame pack (2–9 L)*
5 *Fork pack × 2 (6–8 L)*
6 *Top tube packs × 2 (0.5–1 L)*
7 *Down Tube pack (1–2 L)*
8 *Stem packs × 2 (1–2 L)*
9 *Hip pack (2–6 L)*
= *37 L–76 L*
~~10 Full Pannier Setup (75–105 L)~~

BIKE & SETUP

Several factors have to be considered. Things like bigger tires and lower gearing are essential for heading off-road.

A *Frame material/geometry/specs*
B *Gearing/drivetrain/shifting*
C *Brakes*
D *Wheel and tire size/tread*
E *Handlebars and hand positions*
F *Mounts for racks/cages*
G *Saddle*
H *Navigation/devices*
J *Dynamo hub lighting/charging*
K *Pedals*
L *Mudguards*

BIKEPACKER

BIKE: "All terrain" gravel or mountain
LUGGAGE: Bikepacking bags
TRIPS AND TERRAIN: Roam anywhere. With bigger tires and a nimbler setup, carry everything you need for a few days and reach higher, more remote, and wilder worlds, even if pushing your bike is required. Space can be limited, especially for clunkier items like one-liter, or more, cooking pots and water and food supplies beyond 3–4 days. Tape your frame where bags attach and might rub.

FASTPACKER

BIKE: Road, gravel, or mountain
LUGGAGE: Bikepacking bags
TRIPS AND TERRAIN: Fast and light road and off-road adventures carrying the bare minimum. Typically shorter trips in known weathers, using accommodations. Camping and cooking are seen more as secondary, with only room for a bivvy setup, lightweight stove set, and minimal supplies.

TRADITIONAL TOURER

BIKE: Touring/expedition
LUGGAGE: Traditional pannier bags
TRIPS AND TERRAIN: Road and light off-road adventures, for as long as you want to be away. A full set of panniers not only offers more space to carry whatever you need, but is less fussy to pack and easier to take on and off the bike. However, additional weight does makes the bike less agile across technical off-road terrain—the reason for the development of "rackless" bikepacking bags.

ALTERNATIVES

BIKE: Various
LUGGAGE: Trailers, racks, baskets, backpacks
TRIPS AND TERRAIN: Various. Mix things up! A bikepacker setup with the addition of front panniers or a backpack can carry enough supplies and equipment for a few more days in the wild, and does not affect technical off-road capabilities too much. For adventures with kids, add a trailer to a "fastpacker" setup.

MASTER KITGRID

Self-sufficiency in the world's wilds means each trip calls for a different kit list. Here are the basics to consider:

RIDING CLOTHING

1 *Helmet/cap*
2 *Sunglasses*
3 *Rugged shoes (SPD/flats)*
4 *Socks*
5 *Bib-padded shorts*
6 *Over-shorts*
7 *Base layer*
8 *Shirt/jersey*
9 *Wind/water-proof jacket*
10 *Insulated Layer*
11 *Wind/water-proof pants*
12 *Mitts/gloves*
13 *Buff*

OFF-THE-BIKE CLOTHING

14 *Cozy insu-lated jacket*
15 *Shirt*
16 *Leggings*
17 *Underwear*
18 *Warm hat*
19 *Warm socks*
20 *Shoes/sandals*

SHELTER

21 *Tent*
22 *Sleeping mat/pillow*
23 *Sleeping bag/quilt*

COOKING, WATER, DRINKS, & FOOD

24 *Stove*
25 *Fuel/lighter*
26 *Pot(s)*
27 *Spork/knife*
28 *Mug*
29 *Coffee/tea equipment*
30 *Water filter*

31 *Water bottles/bladder*
32 *Insulated/hip flasks*
33 *Snacks*
34 *Food supplies*
35 *Drink supplies*
36 *Trash bags*

WASHBAG

37 *Toothbrush/toothpaste*
38 *Travel towel*
39 *Tissues/biodegradable wet wipes*
40 *Sunscreen*
41 *Bug/bear spray*
42 *Toilet trowel*

FIRST AID KIT

43 *See "Trail-side Fixes" p.94*

TOOLS & SPARES

44 *See "Trail-side Fixes" p.94*

ELECTRONICS

45 *GPS device*
46 *Smartphone*
47 *Camera*
48 *Front and rear lights*
49 *Headlamp*
50 *USB battery pack/spare batteries*
51 *Wall charger/charging cables*
52 *Headphones*

MISCELLANEOUS

53 *Map/compass*
54 *Sketchbook/pen*
55 *Wallet/passport/insurance*
56 *Cable lock*

RIDING THE LENGTH OF THE RIVER NIDD, IN SEARCH OF TROUT

→

ROUTE
BIKEFISHING NIDDERDALE

LOCATION
ENGLAND

AS THEY WADED upstream, the River Nidd's cold dark waters lapped at David's and Stefan's rolled-up bikepacking shorts with every precarious step over the rocky riverbed. It was early morning in the heart of Yorkshire's Nidderdale, where fly fishing friend and guide Oscar Boatfield is based. Moments ago, he lifted up a peat-covered brown rock to highlight the entomology that fly fishing is largely based around: clinging caddis casings, the first stage of a fly's life, one of the many types of baits that a fly is meant to imitate. Soon after, the casting commenced into the fast-flowing water and pockets where Nidd trout would most likely be hanging out, facing upstream and fighting the current in search of food and oxygenated water.

A popular pursuit already, bike-fishing, and the idea of combining cycling and bikepacking with fishing, has been a leisure mainstay in places like North America and Japan—the originator of a simpler style of fishing known as *tenkara*—for a long time now. However, this trip in Yorkshire was an opportunity to figure it all out, alongside expert fly fisherfolk, in the finest of U.K. riding and fly-fishing playgrounds.

Rewind 24 hours earlier, David, Duncan, and Stefan were loading bikes with overnight and fishing kits (rods, reels, flies, and lines) at the end of the River Nidd, but the start of their bikefishing journey, the confluence with the River Ouse, was in the village of Nun Monkton. Their plan was to retrace the Nidd's waters in the opposite direction, inland and upstream, following the river's farmed floodplains and meandering meadows, past Harrogate, and to end at the spring source on Nidderdale's Area of Natural Beauty's border with the Yorkshire Dales National Park. Along the way, they would pause for upstream fishing in the river and still-water fishing at an upland reservoir, two quite different experiences. Riding north through Nidderdale, the roads would get narrower, the hills higher, the moors wilder, and the river smaller.

The majority of the moorlands that forge the Nidd's stunning ridged watershed are high pastures for sheep, patterned with an array of dry stone walls and stone barns. The group rode tracks alongside farmers on their quad bikes and border collie dogs rounding up scores of sheep. As the last of the sun lit up the now distant dam, the group unpacked and put together their rods, attaching reels and flies. They headed out along the rock groyne—10 meters (33 feet) away from the shoreline—to begin casting. Still-water fishing is a totally different game to river fishing. Due to varying habitats and ecosystems, the fish behave and live differently. They hang out in different places and feed on different things, meaning experience and a bit of luck are needed to figure out patterns. One thing is for sure, there is no better place to learn about rods and casting than a wide open and empty reservoir shoreline. As a beginner, there is a good chance you will cast a hook onto your own clothes at some point.

Regarding rods, there are a couple of formats portable enough for →

"ON A BIKEFISHING TRIP LIKE THIS ALONG THE LENGTH OF A RIVER, YOU WILL RIDE, SWIM, DRINK, WADE, HIKE, AND FISH ITS WATERS."

bikepacking, including traditional fly fishing, with a 2.5–3-meter (9–10-foot) rod and reel/line, or *tenkara,* with a typically much shorter rod and a fixed line that packs down small enough to fit in a hip pack. A traditional setup is great for learning to cast properly, especially for lake and reservoir still-water fishing, which you need a longer line for. *Tenkara* is originally the Japanese term for "fishing from heaven," and this style of rod is used for the popular mountain stream fly fishing

and close-cast fishing in smaller bodies of water. David and Stefan used the more traditional 2.5–3-meter (9–10-foot) rods that break down and can squeeze into a 3-foot carrying tube. There are few options for carrying rods while biking—bar/top tube/fork leg—unless you opt for a *tenkara*-style, which fits onto a hip pack or within a bike bag.

On a bikefishing trip like this along the length of a river, you will ride, swim, drink, wade, hike, and fish its waters. And, yes, the guys only

caught one little trout over two fly-fishing sessions, but that is not the point. The point is the pursuit, and the joy, serenity, and escape, of being immersed in these upland landscapes. As Thoreau said: "Many [people] go fishing all of their lives, without knowing that it is not fish they are after." After a first proper bikefishing experience, it is hard to argue with that.

When you have the chance, strap a fishing rod to your bike and head off bikefishing. ○

THERE ARE A COUPLE
OF FLY-FISHING STYLE
AND ROD OPTIONS:
TRADITIONAL OR
TENKARA. EACH HAVE
THEIR ADVANTAGES.

TYPICAL YORKSHIRE BIKEPACKING LANDSCAPES: UPLAND MOORS WITH A LONG TRADITION OF HILL FARMING.

BIKEPACKING IS AS MUCH ABOUT TIME OFF THE BIKE: INCLUDING AN EXTRA PURSUIT CAN HELP WITH TRIP MOTIVES.

KEY TRIP NOTES

REGION/LOCATION(S):
Yorkshire: Nidderdale Area
of Natural Beauty

CATEGORY:
Overnighter

DISTANCE:
120 km (75 mi)

TERRAIN:
Road/gravel

SKILL LEVEL:
Easy

HIGHLIGHTS:
Kit geekery, upstream river
fishing, upland reservoir
fishing, pub lunches, and
that first bite.

**ESSENTIAL GEAR/
EQUIPMENT:**
Packable fly fishing kit
(fishing rod, fishing reel/
line, flies, river footwear/
sandals), patience.

IMPORTANT INFO:
Before fishing, make sure to
check the rules on fishing in
your location. The waters will
be owned by someone and will
be subject to certain rules and
restrictions. In order to fish
freshwater in the U.K., you
will need an Environmental
Agency Fishing License.

RESUPPLY INFO:
Pateley Bridge. Pubs and
cafes dot the dales, but
double-check openings.

RIDE SEASON:
Year-round. For fly fishing:
March–October

CONTRIBUTOR/RIDER INFO

Bikefishing Nidderdale was
a Pannier.cc production to
learn more about combining
bikepacking and fly fishing.
David Sear, Duncan Philpott,
and Stefan Amato teamed up
with Oscar and Nell Boatfield,
who are experts in the world
of fly fishing and based
in one of the U.K.'s largely
undiscovered secret valleys,
located on the edge of the
Yorkshire Dales National Park.

POINT TOWARD THE BREAK: WAVE HUNTING IN ASTURIAS

→

LOCATION
ASTURIAS, SPAIN

SAMI SAURI AND OLI CULCHETH strained against the weight of their trailers as they stood on pedals and leaned into the loose, dusty climb. Each trailer was stacked with two surfboards and a bag full of wetsuits and fins. Just beyond the hill was the Atlantic Ocean and the stunning Asturias coastline of northern Spain. Known as the Costa Verde, it lived up to its name: vibrant green undergrowth and grasses, studded with yellow wildflowers in full bloom, lined the small roads and rolling gravel tracks.

The group had set off from San Vicente de la Barquera, taking turns to tow the two trailers with Sami and Oli taking the first shifts. Oli felt strong after a week of bike-packing in the nearby Picos d'Europa mountains and Sami was keen to protect the surfboard she had just finished making with her own hands. Amy Brock Morgan and Rémi Clermont rode alongside, unencumbered by the extra weight of surfing equipment, enjoying the relative freedom of riding with just camp gear hanging

from their bikes. Chris McClean might not have had a surfboard to drag, but it is the photographer's lot to always carry a little extra; it was a novelty to not have the most to carry.

The group's plan was to use bikes to explore the harder-to-reach surf spots scattered along the complex coastline of Asturias, meticulously checking coastal maps, weather forecasts, and tide times in search of "blue gold" and perfect playful surf breaks.

Cycling does not seem like the most logical way to travel to the surf, but what is logical about adventure? However, the large overlap of surfers and cyclists is less surprising. After all, bikes and boards are just different tools with which to play in the outdoors. For those that are interested in both cycling and surfing, why not try to combine the two?

At the top of the climb, Sami and Oli might have been able to explain why. Scanning the sea below them, they read the conditions quickly. All obsessions have their own lingo and terminology.

There was no need for a surfer-cyclist dictionary on this occasion. There was no left, right, A-frame, or close out. No lip, peak, pocket, impact zone, or shoulder to analyze. The sea was simply … flat.

The surf might have been nonexistent, but the camp spot was world-class. The group set up home for the evening, sipping martinis on the cliff's edge under fruit salad skies, shades of apricot, peach, and strawberry staining the sea as the light slowly died.

Over the next couple of days the group drifted westward, then back east, chasing surf that always felt just out of reach. They almost forgot the trailers on the flatter sections, freewheeling as they scanned the sea below. There were frequent stops to recheck shipping forecasts and weather maps, and to swap turns hauling the surf gear. It felt as if the trailers were getting heavier and heavier, almost as though the weight of expectation was tucked next to the neoprene wetsuits.

Finally on the last evening, they →

24

EVEN THE EASIEST OF CLIMBS WERE ENERGY-SAPPING WHEN YOU TOWED A LOAD OF SURFING PARAPHERNALIA ALONG BEHIND YOU.

"CYCLING DOES NOT SEEM LIKE THE MOST LOGICAL WAY TO TRAVEL TO THE SURF, BUT WHAT IS LOGICAL ABOUT ADVENTURE?"

returned to San Vicente de la Barquera, sweaty, dusty, and dehydrated—and still surfless. They stocked up on beers and continued farther west, into Oyambre Nature Reserve. Finally, at Playa De Gerra they found surf. The swell at the west-facing bay was not big, but it was, at least, consistent. The conditions were hard work on their short boards and they shared jokes with the locals as they cruised past on longboards, but after days in the saddle, it just felt great to finally be in the water. The objects that had felt like anchors at times were gone and they were now in their element.

It did not matter that they had ridden 120 kilometers (75 miles) to find surf 10 kilometers (6 miles) from their start point. It did not matter that they never found blue gold. Whether it is surfing or riding, the joy of the hunt is not in the catch itself, but the journey to get there. And while cycling was not the most practical mode for the journey, it certainly made the most modest of sea conditions feel more revitalizing than ever. ○

"AFTER ALL, BIKES AND BOARDS ARE JUST DIFFERENT TOOLS WITH WHICH TO PLAY IN THE OUTDOORS."

THE SURF MAY NOT HAVE BEEN ALL-TIME, BUT BEACH-SIDE COFFEES AND MARTINIS SOFTENED ANY DISAPPOINTMENT.

KEY TRIP NOTES

REGION/LOCATION(S):
Asturias sits on the coast of northern Spain and is dotted with hidden surf spots.

CATEGORY:
Out and back bikepacking, long weekender

DISTANCE:
120 km (75 mi)

TERRAIN:
Gentle tarmac and smooth gravel

SKILL LEVEL:
Easy, although it becomes a little harder when you are towing a surfboard and wetsuit.

HIGHLIGHTS:
Cooling down in the surf after a hot day riding and the looks of surprise from locals as you arrive by bike.

ESSENTIAL GEAR/ EQUIPMENT:
Camp gear and for the full experience, a surfboard and trailer to tow it.

RESUPPLY INFO:
There are villages all along the coast.

RIDE SEASON:
Summer

CONTRIBUTOR/RIDER INFO

Sami Sauri, Oli Culcheth, Amy Brock Morgan, and Rémi Clermont are riders and surfers with varying levels of experience. Chris McClean is a professional photographer and filmmaker specializing in surf and cycle.

IN PRAISE OF CITY-TO-CITY WEEKEND ESCAPES

ROUTE
**PEAKLAND & ROUTE
BEER RAMBLES**

LOCATION
ENGLAND

UNLESS YOU were to pick two cities like, say, Geneva and Turin that are divided by the highest mountains in Europe, the simple concept of linking up two cities makes for a great bikepacking adventure. Not only do point-to-point routes have a more rewarding feel, but by utilizing public transport, the major travel logistics are straightforward. It's just a case of planning the best route between cities. More often than not, they will be historically linked by lines of communication, and although many of these will now be major roads or rail routes, there will likely be a network of river or canal ways, quiet tarmac roads, and gravel tracks to be explored. Taking these tracks less

traveled will not be the most direct route, of course, but it makes for a rewarding journey and adventure. Pannier.cc's "rambles"—their term for a city-to-city weekend bikepacking trip—started as a simple documentation of a weekend ride from London to a family friend's brewery in Bristol to taste a batch of the Pannier Route Beer they had made for their events. The following year, they opened the weekend ride up for booking and, since then, rambles have become their most popular bikepacking format. In addition to the Route Beer London-Bristol ramble, they now host a Peakland ramble between Manchester and Sheffield through the Peak District National Park, and are →

PYM CHAIR—THE INFAMOUS
ROAD CLIMB THAT TAKES
YOU FROM MANCHESTER
AND OVER INTO THE PEAK
DISTRICT NATIONAL PARK.

soon launching the South Downs ramble along the South Downs Way from Winchester to Eastbourne, where you can enjoy a swim and fish and chips on the south coast.

The route options from London to Bristol might surprise you. The distance and mixed-terrain possibilities make for an ace adventure. The team at Pannier.cc stitched together a great mix of London Royal Parks, River Thames towpaths, ferry crossings, and mountain bike trail centers, before reaching the bounds of the North Wessex downlands for quiet hedgerow lanes, exposed common tracks, and English village greens. After an overnight camp and a proper meal at a traditional English inn, the ride continues mainly on off-road canal and river paths, pausing only for a cream tea in picturesque Bradford-on-Avon, before heading around historic Bath and finishing up at a brewery in Bristol. Riders are then free to get the train home or stay the night and spend the following day exploring Bristol.

The Peak District National Park is the home playground of Pannier.cc, so hosting a bikepacking weekend between the northern powerhouse cities of Manchester and Sheffield was a no-brainer. Beginning with early morning coffees and a briefing in Manchester, the route follows the canal and bridleway network, leaving the urban towers and bustle behind, before reaching the countryside and hills at Lyme Park. Heading east through Macclesfield Forest, along exposed ridgeline gravel tracks, the route then heads past gin distilleries, up category climbs, and along stunning Peak District moor-land lanes. A stay at a joyous pub near Bakewell caps off the day. At the halfway point, fuel up on a traditional Derby-shire oatcake brekky at Pannier.cc's favorite cafe in Monyash, and then head through the rolling limestone tracks and old rail trails of the White Peak. The route joins the ancient trade route from Manchester to Sheffield through the Hope Valley and up amongst the famous gritstone edges of the Dark Peak. Here, riders are rewarded with a 10-kilometer (6-mile) freewheel descent into Sheffield. After-wards, riders are then free to get the train home or stay the night and spend the following day exploring Sheffield.

A weekend riding between two cities is a great reminder that wild, epic locations are not the be-all and end-all. Bikepacking is as much a tool for discovering new places and spending time with like-minded people. Riding in typically fewer remote places is a great way to start bikepacking: resupply is not an issue, places like pubs and cafes to eat and socialize in are widely available, and while the likelihood of things not going to plan is always a possibility, you definitely have more chances of turning it around.

Top tips for planning a weekend ramble? Gather a friend, or a few friends. Pick two interesting and accessible cities that are a comfortable distance apart. While riding on mixed-terrain, on and off-road, expect to cover anywhere between 5–15 kilometers (3–9 miles) per hour, so aim to cover anywhere between 50–150 kilometers (30–90 miles) per day, depending on your confidence level and experience. Sometimes a great way to start is to pick a city you can get to by train that is a set distance from where you live and ride home. The end goal is easy to visualize that way. Look for any established cycling routes that already exist between the two. Seek out points of interest and overnight accommo-dation options and plot a route. Sometimes it is a good idea to front-load the distance on the first day to make the second day more relaxed. Stock up on food and drink supplies before setting off, but always leave room in your bags for picking up things you might find along the way. Always note backup options along the route, or nearby, just in case. Other things like knowing where the train stations or major towns and villages are are also always useful.

It cannot get easier and more accessible—all year round. What two cities could you link up? ○

THE SOCIAL SIDE OF BIKEPACKING IS WHAT IT'S ABOUT—RIDING AS A GROUP, AND ENJOYING EVENINGS UNDER THE STARS.

"A WEEKEND RIDING BETWEEN TWO CITIES IS A GREAT REMINDER THAT WILD, EPIC LOCATIONS ARE NOT THE BE-ALL AND END-ALL."

KEY TRIP NOTES

REGION/LOCATION(S):
London-Bristol (North Wessex downlands), Manchester-Sheffield (Peak District National Park)

CATEGORY:
Weekend-overnighters

DISTANCE:
150–250 km (93–155 mi)

TERRAIN:
Road/gravel

SKILL LEVEL:
Easy–intermediate

HIGHLIGHTS:
Escaping the city, pub overnights, ferry crossings, forest trails, moorland tracks, and group social riding.

ESSENTIAL GEAR/ EQUIPMENT:
Snacks and water bottles, waterproof clothing, lights (it is easy to get caught out in the dark, especially in winter), and camping kit if you cannot locate fixed accommodations.

RESUPPLY INFO:
Stock up before you leave London or Manchester. Riding between cities in the U.K. is rarely remote, and there are plenty of small shops to stock up along the way. It is worth checking out potential pit stops before setting off, as certain sections can be sparse.

RIDE SEASON:
Year-round

CONTRIBUTOR / RIDER INFO

Pannier.cc is a bikepacking tour operator based in the U.K., but hosts experiences much further afield, from U.K. weekend rambles to three- to four-day escapes in the Bjelašnica mountains of Bosnia and bucket-list expeditions like the Annapurna Circuit in Nepal.

A S240 SCHOOL NIGHT GRAVEL ESCAPE IN CENTRAL GERMANY

→

ROUTE
FRANCONIA BACKLANDS

LOCATION
GERMANY

FORGET THE 9 to 5; 5 to 9 is where the adventure lies.

It was autumn and the height of pumpkin season in the Franconian backlands. Vast piles of picked pumpkins lined the dusty farm tracks and dry forest trails that Peter Wöstmann, Volker Haug, Scot Easter, Nils Amelinckx, and Stefan sped along, into the slowly setting sun, en route to a cooperative-owned forest hut around 50 kilometers (30 miles) away, directly west of Heilsbronn.

The pandemic's pause in national and international travel has definitely put local adventure back on the map—and for good reason. It is all too easy to look further afield and ignore your own backyard when it comes to bike escapes. For these guys, who were in Heilsbronn on work duties, the biking playgrounds of the Black Forest and Bavarian Alps loomed on their radar. But following a busy day at cycling company Ortlieb's headquarters and factory, learning about heritage and manufacuring, and repairing the bike-packing bags everyone had strapped to their bikes, a simple overnighter

proved the power of escape, adventure, and community that bikes enable. There are no big landscapes around this part of Germany, but there are big blue skies, plenty of fun farm and flowy forest tracks to enjoy, and more than enough distance for a challenging evening and morning out together. And that is the idea with overnight 5 to 9 escapes—or an S24O (sub 24-hour-overnighter), as they are commonly known in the bikepacking world. They are opportunistic, accessible adventures that fit in with the routine and constraints of modern day life. Wild and epic is not the point. Dream big, start small. But start. You will rarely regret it.

Nils lit the fire straight after arriving, as the sun set a big, bright orange over the tiny village horizon. Thirst and hunger were a priority after a speedy 50 kilometers (30 miles) in the evening sun, but first, while the fire started roaring, it was time to unpack the bikes and set up sleeping mats and bags before sitting around the chunky wooden table to prep food over drinks and future trip discussions. Since it was pumpkin

season, and Stefan having carried one all the way from Heilsbronn, the group ceremoniously carved the giant squash before wrapping it in foil with a sprinkling of feta to roast on the embers. Although pumpkin works well in pasta, as a soup, or chunked up in a one-pot camp stew, this trip was about keeping things simple. On the menu was a whole host of other vegetable and meat barbeque options, including the local delicacy: *Drei im Weggla,* the "three in a bun" Franconian hot dog. After a big meal, local beers, and some decent kilometers in the legs, the group was more than ready to retire into the hut for the warmth and comfort of sleeping bags as the embers just about stopped glowing in the light breeze. Since everyone needed to be back in Heilsbronn for work at 9 a. m., it would be an early start the next morning, but they would still make time at dawn to have a camp coffee, a quick shower, and to change out of sweaty and smokey kit—the sign of a good evening and morning on the bikes!

Happy to have sneaked in this adventure. Where could you escape on an S240? ○

AS GREAT AS
BREWING DAWN
DRINKS AT CAMP IS,
SUSS OUT THE BEST
CAFE FOR A PROPER
FEED AND COFFEE
BEFORE WORK!

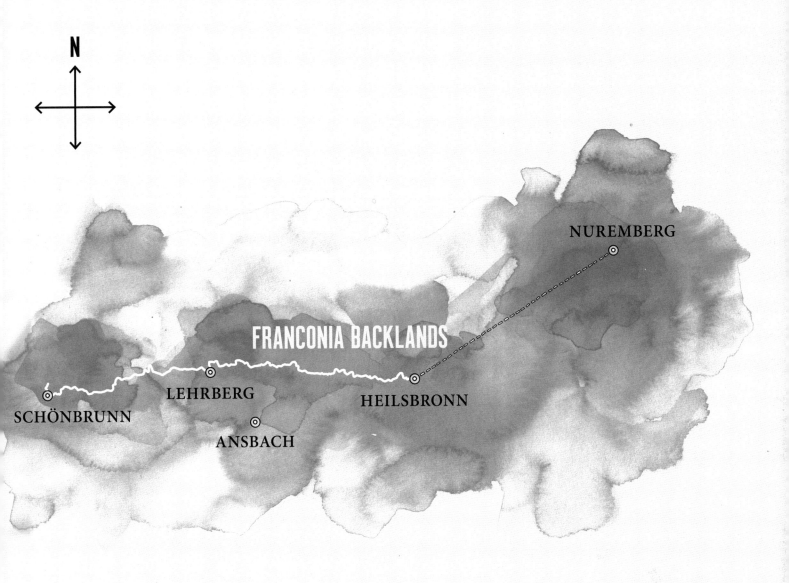

N

NUREMBERG

FRANCONIA BACKLANDS

LEHRBERG

HEILSBRONN

SCHÖNBRUNN

ANSBACH

KEY TRIP INFO

REGION/LOCATION(S):
Franconia
CATEGORY:
S240-overnighter
DISTANCE:
100 km (62 mi)
TERRAIN:
Road/gravel
SKILL LEVEL:
Easy

HIGHLIGHTS:
Cooking outdoors, sampling local food and drink, waking up under the stars, and racing back to work.
ESSENTIAL GEAR/EQUIPMENT:
Camping kit, barbeque supplies, morning coffee kit, wash kit, and a range of clothes for the next work day.
RESUPPLY INFO:
Heilsbronn
RIDE SEASON:
Year-round

CONTRIBUTOR/RIDER INFO

The Franconia Backlands trip was a Pannier.cc production with the guys at cycling company Ortlieb, whose head office and factory is in Heilsbronn. Joining Stefan were Peter Wöstmann, Volker Haug, Nils Amelinckx, and Scot Easter. Accessible overnight escapes like this are just the tonic, especially mid-week.

TWELVE RIDERS STRAIGHT TO THE HEART OF PORTLAND

→

ROUTE
**SEATTLE TO
PORTLAND**

LOCATION
**PACIFIC NORTHWEST,
UNITED STATES**

NEVER IS the truism "life is about the journey, not the destination" more accurate than when bikepacking. They set off with an end point in mind, but the defining moments on a ride so often end up being the unplanned and unexpected moments along the way.

Twelve riders met in downtown Seattle, Washington, with the objective of riding to the Radical Adventure Riders' WTF Bikexplorer's Summit, traveling the 500 kilometers (311 miles) to Portland, Oregon, on gravel roads over five days.

Not everyone knew each other at the start, but they all had at least two things in common. Firstly, they were all involved in the bicycle community in one way or another, from career bike mechanics and grassroots event organizers to guides, salespeople, and independent business owners. Each and every one shows up every day to get work done in the bike industry. Secondly, none of them identify as cis-male.

The dozen-strong crew of non-binary, trans, queer, and female-identified people rode out from downtown Seattle with the wild ambitions of talking about industry change, sharing the shit they had to deal with in the cycling world, and working out how to best support each other's work. To be honest, they never really seemed to find the time to talk shop. Instead, they cooked together, tackled the route's steep climbs together, snored side by side, and, in their words, "had a gay old time." And they did so in an environment free from the bias, bigotry, preconceptions, and prejudice they all experienced in their everyday lives.

The route took them directly south, through the suburbs of Seattle, before hitting dirt on the outskirts with Mount Rainier visible far in the distance beyond. On their second day, they tickled the edges of the mountain's national park as rain showers blew through. Mist entangled itself on treetops like wisps of cotton candy and the smell of petrichor hung in the humid air as the rain hit warm tarmac.

The sun returned on the third day, while they downed espressos from a wooden shack next to Trout Lake General Store, before strapping six-packs of beers to their bikes →

FROM CITY TO WILDERNESS,
TO CITY IN 500 KM. PORTLAND,
OREGON MIGHT HAVE BEEN
THEIR DESTINATION, BUT IT
WAS FAR FROM THE END OF
THE JOURNEY.

"THE DEFINING MOMENTS ON A RIDE SO OFTEN END UP BEING THE UNPLANNED AND UNEXPECTED ONES."

and swimming in Takhlakh Lake under the snow-capped Mount Adams. The group finally made camp in the woods just south of the lake, where they hung their clothes on a washing line between the trees alongside bunting that looked like a rainbow of primary colors fluttering in the gentle breeze. Tents and hammocks surrounded the old picnic table—with benches that sagged wildly in the middle—where they laughed and told jokes, shared tall tales, and had heartfelt conversations long into the evening.

Sun beat down on the riders' backs as they broke camp and winched their way up climbs that were so steep and long they tackled them in pitches, weaving across the dirt roads to lessen the gradient and seek out grip in the dust and loose gravel. As they climbed higher, more and more layers of landskein—a word to describe the weaving and braiding of horizon lines—were revealed: peaks, forested ridgelines, and mountain flanks laying beyond the trailside foxgloves.

On the final day they crossed the Oregon state boundary on a bike path running down the center of Route 205, straight in the heart of Portland. Cars flashed by as the crew crossed the Columbia River, ready to join the WTF Bikexplorer's Summit. Their destination had been reached, but rather than being the end point, it was a starting point for the journeys of the capable, kind, gentle, and insanely strong crew that had already ridden this far together. ○

"HAVING A GAY OLD TIME," FROM DODGING RAIN SHOWERS TO LONG EVENINGS IN CAMP.

KEY TRIP NOTES

REGION/LOCATION(S):
Pacific Northwest

CATEGORY:
Multiday mixed-terrain bike camping trip with friends

DISTANCE:
500 km (311 mi)

TERRAIN:
Gravel and surfaced roads

SKILL LEVEL:
Advanced. The amount of climbing means the route is a tough one for the distance.

HIGHLIGHTS:
Linking two cities via Mount Rainier National Park and its surrounding Takhlakh Lake and Gifford Pinchot National Forest.

ESSENTIAL GEAR/ EQUIPMENT:
Camp gear and water filter. Given the amount of climbing, you will be thankful for the weight-saving approach of bringing a filter rather than liters of water.

RESUPPLY INFO:
Daily resupplies, but they can be spread out. There is up to 100 km (62 mi) between towns.

RIDE SEASON:
July–October

CONTRIBUTOR/RIDER INFO

Gritchelle Fallesgon is a professional photographer based in Portland. She was joined on this trip by Kai Condradi, Amanda Bryan, Donald Villareal, Ellie Kaszniak, Jenny Schmidt, Martina Brimmer, Pepper Cook, Sam Saarni, Everett Ó Cillín, Tessa Hulls, and Mo.

SEEKING FRILUFTSLIV ON THE BLEKINGELEDEN

ROUTE
BLEKINGELEDEN / SKÅNELEDEN

LOCATION
SWEDEN

IT WAS THE TAIL end of a long day of riding, pushing, carrying bikes over stiles, and then finally swimming in the sea to wash away the dirt and sweat of hours in (and out) of the saddle. Sabina Knezevic and Robin Patijn sat in sleeping bags watching the sun set over the Baltic Sea. There is always something magical about the fleeting moments when fire meets water. Each moment is uniquely transient and no less spectacular regardless of how many times you find yourself looking west at dusk. In front of them: high cliffs and steep ravines down to fjords. Surrounding the pair: a *vindskydd* or lean-to. The three-sided log cabins are located at regular

intervals along the 270-kilometer (168-mile) Blekingeleden, and Sabina and Robin made the most of the basic shelters as they rode the length of the trail that follows the southern coast of Sweden. Each night they would light a campfire in the designated pits and grill sausages and toast marshmallows before falling asleep listening to the embers hiss as they cooled.

The Blekingeleden—*leden* means "trail" in Swedish—turned out to be a stunning trail that offered a varied surface along paths and gravel roads, cutting through forests, pastures, lakes, and fields. The riders set off from the medieval town Sölvesborg in →

the west of Blekinge, following gentle gravel that lured them into a false sense of security. Surely it would not take long to traverse the entire length of the trail? It did not take long for them to revise their expectations. The Blekingeleden was designed as a hiking trail originally, and significant sections are not wholly rideable. Rooty singletrack and slippery, moss-covered rocks forced them to spend more time pushing their bikes than either Sabina or Robin wanted. It was frustrating

initially, but it did not take long for them to readjust and enjoy a slower pace of life. It was 2020, and simply being in the woods felt like a privilege and a release after months of living within the restrictions of a pandemic.

The Swedes have a word for the sense of connectedness to nature, and the well-being it brings. They call it *friluftsliv*. In English, it means "outdoor life," or literally, "free air life." The tradition of *friluftsliv* is even written into the Swedish constitution: "Alla ska ha tillgång

till naturen"—everyone shall have access to nature. This constitutional right to public access invites everyone to roam free. As long as you do not disturb or destroy, you can pretty much swim, walk, ski, boat, run, and even go berry picking just about anywhere. It is thanks to this constitution that there are over 3,000 *vindskydd* in the country. Virtually every cyclist would identify with the concept of *friluftsliv* if asked about it. Although we may not always appreciate the

"THE SWEDES HAVE A WORD FOR THE SENSE OF CONNECTEDNESS TO NATURE, AND THE WELL-BEING IT BRINGS. THEY CALL IT 'FRILUFTSLIV'."

CYCLING SWEDISH TRAILS OFTEN MEANS YOU HAVE TO CARRY YOUR BIKE OVER OBSTACLES. HAVING A MINIMALISTIC BIKEPACKING SETUP CAN BE LIBERATING.

simple joy of being outdoors as much as we could. It is easy to take it for granted until circumstances take it away.

Berries and coffee make a great breakfast, especially when eaten in a sleeping bag while you watch the sunlight creeping toward you and listen to the forest waking up. It would be tempting to remain in the same spot for the rest of the day, but every morning the pair awoke re-energized, closer to the environment that they had slept in and keen to see more.

After breaking camp, Sabina and Robin would get moving, sometimes cruising along gravel that served as an even better pick-me-up than the coffee. Other times they would find themselves sliding down dew-covered roots, waiting for their brains to catch up with the task at hand. Breaks would be dictated by the availability of lakes for swimming and clearings in the trees with scenic views out to sea. They meandered through the coastal region, but regularly turned inland

through rolling hills and thick hardwood forests where the sun barely penetrated, even at the height of midday.

When they eventually arrived at the finish in Bröms, at the most northeastern tip of the province, the pair felt tired but lifted by their experience and better able to process the wider events of the world. The ride had been an escape, but more than that, it had been a reconnection to what they loved. Sabina and Robin had found *friluftsliv*. ○

"VIRTUALLY EVERY
CYCLIST WOULD
IDENTIFY WITH
THE CONCEPT OF
'FRILUFTSLIV' IF
ASKED ABOUT IT."

THE RIGHT OF PUBLIC ACCESS,
OR "ALLEMANSRÄTTEN" IN
SWEDISH, INVITES EVERYONE TO
ROAM FREE AND EXPLORE THE
BEAUTY OF THE COUNTRY.

KEY TRIP NOTES

REGION/LOCATION(S):
Blekinge is often described as the southernmost wilderness in Sweden.

CATEGORY:
2–3 day escape

DISTANCE:
270 km (168 mi)

TERRAIN:
Everything from easy gravel to technical mountain bike singletrack.

SKILL LEVEL:
Advanced. A more challenging trail than the distance and 2,200 meter (7,218 feet) of height gain/loss suggests. Around 70 percent rideable with long sections of walking.

HIGHLIGHTS:
Wild swimming along the way, variety of terrain, and discovering *friluftsliv* for yourself.

ESSENTIAL GEAR/ EQUIPMENT:
Camp gear (although you can leave the tent at home, thanks to the *vindskydd),* cooking supplies, sufficient food, and cycling shoes that are comfortable to hike in.

RESUPPLY INFO:
Make sure to bring enough food for the ride. Although the Blekingetrail leads through many small settlements, shops to stock up at are scarce.

RIDE SEASON:
May–September

CONTRIBUTOR/RIDER INFO

Sabina Knezevic and Robin Patijn are always in search of "Farawayistan," a far away destination that exists only beyond country borders. The suffix -stan is derived from the Persian translation for "place" or "country." They document their trips in the hope of inspiring cyclists all over the world.

TWO FRIENDS DISCOVER OVERLOOKED ROUTES

ROUTE
BLACK FOREST AND ROUTE DU VIN

LOCATION
GERMANY / FRANCE

SO OFTEN WHEN we ride, we are following a specific route. That route may take the form of a GPX file on our bike computer, a highlighted line on a map, or just a mental picture created from years of knowledge of an area. There is a lot to be said for using a route—it helps us avoid getting lost if nothing else—but sometimes it is worth following your nose.

Two friends, Erwin Sikkens and Bas Rotgans, traveled to the south of Germany to spend 11 days exploring the Black Forest and surrounding area. Despite being relatively close to home, neither had thought to ride there before, always lured by adventures farther afield. It was time to fill the gap in their knowledge.

The pair set off with a loose plan to head south to the banks of the Rhine and then make a decision on the best way to return. Riding under pine, oak, and elm trees, canopies of leaves shaded them from the mid-summer sun and their pace was always relaxed. There was always time to sit in the shade of a tree for a while or simply to see what was around the corner before continuing on their way.

Each evening Erwin and Bas would find a *Schutzhütte* (mountain cabin) to rest in. The huts are free to use and open to the public, providing basic shelter from the elements. Most are simple wood constructions with an open side. They would sit, looking →

THE SO-CALLED "SCHUTZHÜTTEN" IN THE BLACK FOREST PROVIDE SHELTER DURING UNSTABLE WEATHER CONDITIONS AND DURING THE NIGHT.

out into the dark forest, and listen to evening rain showers gently drum on the roof, the sound deadened against the thick timber.

The route climbs to the highest point of the Black Mountains. The Feldberg stands at around 1,500 meters (4,921 feet) high and gives long views out to the rolling hills below. Reaching the top late in the afternoon, the pair kept as much height as possible, traversing the mountain and finding another *Schutzhütte* as

the evening air began to chill and the light drained from the sky, but not before painting it with pastel oranges and pinks.

Upon reaching Switzerland and the Rhine, a decision needed to be made: ride back north through the Black Forest, take the easy road via the flat Rhine Valley, or cross over to France and return through the Vosges mountains. They chose the third option. No longer shaded by the forest, →

CROSSING INTO FRANCE MEANT HOT, BURNING SUN WITHOUT A LOT OF FOREST SHADOW. RESOLUTE COOLING DOWN TECHNIQUES WERE NEEDED.

BLACK FOREST RIVER CROSSING NEAR THE FELDBERG.

riding in the Vosges was hot work following white gravel roads through vineyards. In a beautiful mountain refuge, the pair bumped into a French group celebrating a 50th birthday. As is the French way, they shared their wine, food, and fire, and they all stayed up late into the evening sharing tales.

The next few days were spent on the Route du Vin—and it lived up to its name. The pair slept in vineyards, rode more gravel lined with grapevines ripe for picking, and sampled the local produce at the end of each day, their riding kit white with dust and dried sweat.

Finally, as time ran out, the twosome dropped into the Rhine Valley, passing through Strasbourg, and crossed the border back into Germany, completing their clockwise loop.

By simply following their noses, Erwin and Bas discovered new landscapes without the pressure of a flashing line on a GPS device or the counting down of a clock. Almost two weeks had passed. Some days the kilometer count barely ticked over into double figures, while on other days they made large leaps along the trail, fitting the pace to their mood and energy. The result was a route that was worth repeating, and a fuller sense of how their path fit into the landscape that shaped their experience. ○

HOT DAYS AND
A LOT OF STEEP
LITTLE CLIMBS IN
THE ALSACE.

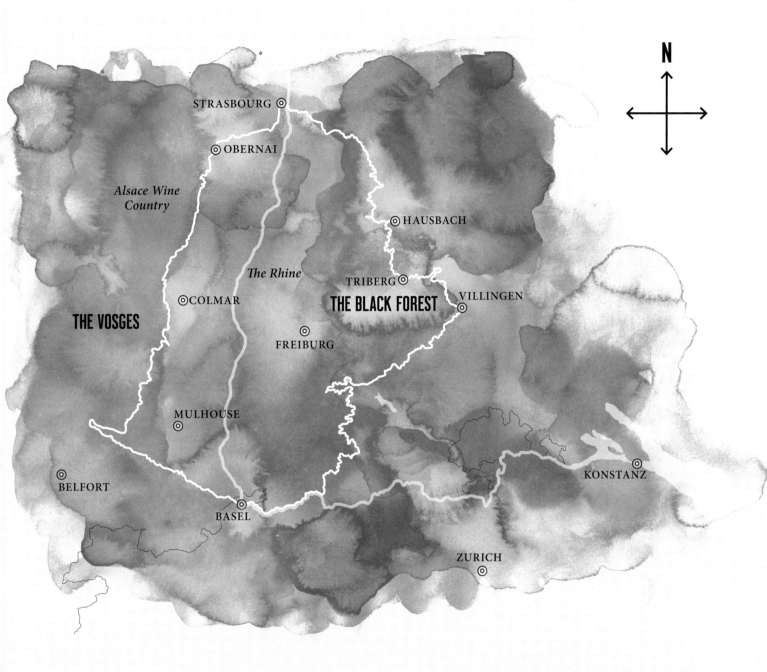

N

STRASBOURG
⊙ OBERNAI
Alsace Wine Country
The Rhine
⊙ HAUSBACH
TRIBERG ⊙ COLMAR
THE BLACK FOREST
⊙ VILLINGEN
THE VOSGES
⊙ FREIBURG
MULHOUSE
KONSTANZ
BELFORT
BASEL
ZURICH

KEY TRIP NOTES

REGION/LOCATION(S):
The Black Forest is a region in the
southwest of Germany. It is bounded
by the Rhine and the Swiss border
to the south and the Vosges mountains
in the west. The forest is crisscrossed
with gravel tracks and country roads,
giving endless opportunities to explore.
The foothills of the Vosges mountains
of France make up part of the Alsace
winemaking region.

CATEGORY:
Multiday, "party pace wins the race,"
improvised route, and circular route

DISTANCE:
610 km (379 mi)

TERRAIN:
Gravel tracks and undulating,
quiet country roads

SKILL LEVEL:
Easy. The route can be made more
challenging by covering more distance
each day or picking more climbing.
In general though, the climbs are
gentle and there is no need to push
hard if you want to take your time
and enjoy the experience.

HIGHLIGHTS:
An unexplored area with some of
the best gravel in Europe, and
amazingly diverse landscapes in
a small geographical area.

ESSENTIAL GEAR/EQUIPMENT:
Standard camp gear. A tent/shelter

isn't needed if you plan on using forest
Schutzhütten and refuges (huts that are
left open and are free to use).

RESUPPLY INFO:
Ample opportunities to resupply all
along the route

RIDE SEASON:
Spring–Autumn

CONTRIBUTOR/RIDER INFO

Erwin Sikkens and Bas Rotgans live in
Germany and the Netherlands. They
had driven through the Black Forest
plenty of times on their way to the Alps,
but had never thought to ride there
until the pandemic forced them to look
for an adventure a little closer to home.

HEBRIDES HOPPING TO JURA, OFF SCOTLAND'S WEST COAST

→

ROUTE
THE LONG ROAD

LOCATION
SCOTLAND

KNITTING TOGETHER five ferry routes—on different days of the week, including the sporadic Sunday service—means diligently noting down 10 timetables, because if there is one takeaway from island-hopping trips, it's that no ferry means you are stuck. Do not expect to have 5G to check a ferry time from a remote pass or slipway, and definitely do not expect ferries to wait for you! However, ferry-hops in this special part of Scotland's west coast are well worth the level of admin for the escape factor. The smell of salty winds and the sound of choppy seas are signs of heading somewhere new.

Sections of the established Kintyre Way—a fully waymarked hiking and biking trail that crisscrosses the Kintyre peninsula for 160 kilometers (100 miles)—formed the first route line, taking the group off the beaten path through forest and moorland estates to the high ridgeline that runs the center of the peninsula and offers views of Jura, Islay, Cara, Gigha, and Arran's craggy mountains to the east. The standout moments were rock pool hike-a-bikes, forest tracks through vast wind farms across breezy ridge tops, an oak-aged gin tasting at Beinn an Tuirc Distillery, and a morning

spent at Bagh na Doirlinne of the Twin Beaches on the Isle of Gigha, where Chris McNally and Stefan took some time out after a beach burrito breakfast to sketch the view across to the Paps of Jura.

There is only one road on Jura. The Long Road, as it has been coined, runs the length of the south and east coast and is a route that has been well-established for centuries. Pieced together over time, the road starts life at the modest port slipway at Feolin, before threading its way between cliff and shore, and across grassy moorlands, dissecting Craighouse—the one and only settlement with any amenities on the island—and heading north for 52 kilometers (32 miles) to nothingness. This nothingness is summed up nicely by one of Stefan's idols, illustrator Alfred Wainwright: "Jura is the loneliest of islands … most of the island is a wilderness—a vast deer forest, scattered habitations, with an inaccessible west coast of cliffs and caves." Much of Jura's history is lore and word of mouth, and its distinct lack of route options certainly lends itself to a land of myth and legend. Following long periods of Norse and inter-clan rivalries, peace has prevailed on Jura, with the population reaching a peak of 1,300 in the 1800s. Although only a short

ferry-hop across the sound from Islay, Jura feels completely detached from the mainland. The distance almost feels swimmable—apparently back in the day cattle used to swim it—but sit out the wait for a ferry and you will be able to stock up at the local store, have a quick drink at the hotel, and watch the crab fishermen at work while the Paps of Jura loom from a shrouding mist beyond.

Like the travelers of old, the group made their way between four change houses (inns) along the Long Road, first to Craighouse and the Jura Hotel, on the seafront with views back over to mainland Kintyre.

Once home to the island's mill, which was built by the Campbell clan in 1775, a blacksmiths forge, telephone exchange, and distillery, the settlement is now home to the Jura Hotel, Jura Distillery, Jura Store, and its own well-equipped campsite.

As the early morning light rose, Craighouse fishermen began heading out in their rowboats to check their pots, while the group prepped a traditional Scottish porridge for breakfast. After stocking up on more crucial Scottish ride snacks (the soft drink Irn-Bru and Tunnock's teacakes) and dinner supplies (pasta, hot smoked salmon, and cabbage) at the quaint →

A FERRY CROSSING CAN
ADD A REAL DISCONNECTION
FACTOR, AND OFTEN
MEANS LOCAL SEAFOOD IS
AVAILABLE TO COOK UP.

"THE LONG ROAD RUNS THE LENGTH OF THE SOUTH AND EAST COAST AND IS A ROUTE THAT HAS BEEN WELL-ESTABLISHED FOR CENTURIES."

Jura stores, the group continued north out of the town for their next peek of the Paps—the rounded quartzite lumps and scree that have been deposited, cooked, hardened, raised, tilted, and sculpted by glacial action. Onwards they rode, rounding bays, to the next checkpoint at Lagg. The last few kilometers to the end of the Long Road are along a fantastic unsurfaced double-track road to Barnhill, where apparently George Orwell camped out to write *1984*. You will see why it might make a good writing haven. There are zero distractions here, just desolate moorlands, deer, ticks, and crashing waves.

After a shared sup on the bottle of Jura Journey, the group decided to retreat for a night at infamous Midge Bay.

At the Jura Hotel, you can read about Midge Bay and the seventeenth-century clan rivalry between the Macleans and Campbells. Lore states that during one raid, the Campbells slipped past the Macleans' watchmen and bound up a lone watchman they encountered in Ardlussa Bay. In such a lonely spot, infested with midges, he was left to die, and it has been called the Bay of Midges since. What better place to spend the last evening of a Hebridean bikepack adventure? ○

THE LONG ROAD

NORTHWESTERN JURA IS AN ALLURING AND STUNNING BUT WILD AND INHOSPITABLE AREA TO EXPLORE, ESPECIALLY BY BIKE.

KEY TRIP NOTES

REGION/LOCATION(S):
Inner Hebrides islands

CATEGORY:
3–4 day escape

DISTANCE:
200 km (125 mi)

TERRAIN:
Road/gravel

SKILL LEVEL:
Easy–intermediate

HIGHLIGHTS:
Ferry-hopping, white sand beaches, distilleries, seafood meals, and nothingness.

ESSENTIAL GEAR/ EQUIPMENT:
Ferry timetables, camping and cooking kits, midge protection, and tick tweezers.

RESUPPLY INFO:
Ayr (mainland), Brodick (Arran), Skipness, Gigha stores, Port Askaig (Islay), Craighouse (Jura). Not much in-between.

RIDE SEASON:
Year-round. Make sure to check ferry services and timetables.

CONTRIBUTOR/RIDER INFO

The Grinduro cycling event was the reason this motley crew was on the Isle of Arran together. After meeting in San Francisco earlier that year, U. S.-based illustrator Chris McNally and Stefan floated the idea of making more of a bikepacking trip, settling on hopping to Kintyre, Gigha, and Jura. Joining for various sections were Chris McClean (photographer), Robin Sansom, Will Meyer, Wren McNally, and Fiola Foley.

OFF THE BEATEN TRACK BETWEEN TWO WHISKY DISTILLERIES

→

ROUTE
DISTILLERY DROVING

LOCATION
SCOTLAND

NESTLED INTO Dumgoyne Hill, the Glengoyne Distillery is a mere 25 kilometers (16 miles) from Glasgow, and yet has a lot of charm. With its miniature glen and hidden waterfall, it is clear to see why George Connell chose this area in 1820 as the ideal location to distil in secret. He eventually gained a license in 1833 and distilled officially, the name not changing to Glengoyne until 1907.

This area is still the Scottish Lowlands, but the Highlands lurk alluringly on the horizon. Riding north, you will cross the Highland Boundary Fault around Aberfoyle, which is where your surroundings really start to change due to collisions between ancient continents 400 million years ago, when the mountains in much of the Highlands rose and the Central Lowlands sank. This fault line created not only the most important geological division in Scotland, but its greatest cultural boundary too. The route north, piecing together some of the West Highland Way and Rob Roy Way, was largely created by the military, drovers, and travelers for the purpose of accessing the Highlands and traveling to and from the more

populated Lowlands. Beneath Glyn Teifi-Jones, Jordan Gibbons, and Stefan's fresh tire tracks were the foot- and hoofprints of Scottish outlaws, folk heroes, and the thousands of drovers and cattle that once journeyed from the Highlands and islands to the markets in Falkirk, across these once trackless wild lands.

Drove roads are widely known as the oldest thoroughfares and route network in Britain. Between the Middle Ages and the industrial revolution, the roads linked the wild corners of Britain in order to supply the growing urban centers. A typical daily drove would cover 16–19 kilometers (10–12 miles), with journeys to the main markets taking anywhere up to a month through all weathers. Droving was a tough, intrepid, and essential trade. In addition to the drove routes, during the 1700s, a network of around 1,700 kilometers (1,050 miles) of military roads was built by Generals Wade and Caulfield to allow government forces to access key locations in the Highlands in case of Jacobite uprisings. There were often pre-existing tracks along →

SCOTTISH SKI CENTERS? OH YES. THERE ARE A FEW, AND GLENCOE BOASTS A CAFE, BASIC ACCOMMODATION AND TRAIL CENTER.

"THE WEST HIGHLAND WAY SECTION FROM BRIDGE OF ORCHY TO FORT WILLIAM HAS TO BE SOME OF THE BEST OFF-ROAD RIDING IN THE UNITED KINGDOM— OR ANYWHERE."

many of the routes made by drovers and travelers, and some of them were used and improved by the military roads. However, new stretches were made where deemed necessary, like the West Highland Way's zigzagging path from Devil's Staircase to Kinlochleven. In 1803, the government improved communications further via the Commissioners for Highland Roads and Bridges, recruiting Scottish civil engineer Thomas Telford to build new roads and bridges in the Highlands, which again helped knit together a lot of this route.

The West Highland Way section from Bridge of Orchy, through Glen Coe and Kinlochleven, to Fort William, has to be some of the best off-road riding in the United Kingdom—or anywhere. Expect fun riding across wide-open moorland among big surrounding peaks, old stone bridges over small brooks and gorges, ruins, ski centers, old traveler pubs and inns, single-track descents, and a small section of hike-a-bike.

After three bumpy days on the road, the miniature bottles of Glengoyne had just about made it intact to Fort William and looked all the more authentic for it. A Glengoyne and Ben Nevis Distillery taste test was on the cards on the train back south. Peer out the train window, and you'll relish retracing tire tracks, but also seeking out new routes. One thing was clear: whatever the reason behind the original lines of communication, adventure cyclists owe a lot to the people who established, trod, built, and maintained the roads and tracks that enable access to these stunning places. The increasingly popular breed of gravel and adventure bikes are the ideal machines for this type of trip, but without any sort of basic track, cyclists would be walking most of the way.

Which established bikepacking route could you make your own? ○

THE WEST HIGHLAND WAY TRACKS THROUGH GLEN COE, BEFORE HEADING UP DEVIL'S STAIRCASE TO GET TO FORT WILLIAM.

DROVE ROADS ARE SEEN
AS THE OLDEST ROUTE
NETWORK IN THE UK.
GLENCOE'S (1786) IS A
SPECIAL OFF-ROAD
RIDING EXPERIENCE.

FORT WILLIAM
Ben Nevis Distillery

KINLOCHLEVEN

Glen Coe

TYNDRUM

LOCH LOMOND
& TROSSACHS
NATIONAL PARK

CALLANDER

ABERFOYLE

Glengoyne distillery

MILNGAVIE

GLASGOW

KEY TRIP NOTES

REGION/LOCATION(S):
Southern Scottish Highlands:
Loch Lomond, Trossachs
National Park, and Glen Coe

CATEGORY:
2–3 day escape

DISTANCE:
200 km (125 mi)

TERRAIN:
Road/gravel

SKILL LEVEL:
Intermediate

HIGHLIGHTS:
Distilleries and whisky tasting, Glen
Coe and Glencoe Drover's Road, Devil's

Staircase, stag spotting, and
finishing drinks at the Grog & Gruel
in Fort William.

ESSENTIAL GEAR/EQUIPMENT:
Camping kit, waterproof clothing,
midge protection, space for whisky
miniatures, and hiking shoes.

RESUPPLY INFO:
Glasgow, Aberfoyle, Tyndrum,
Kinlochleven, and Fort William. It is
worth stocking up on the basics before
you set off, as sections do become
remote. Camping, including wild
camping, is permitted along the route,
but there are a few accommodation
options. Check opening times in
these parts during the off-season.

RIDE SEASON:
March–November

CONTRIBUTOR/RIDERS INFO

Distillery Droving was a Pannier.cc
production initially inspired while
Stefan and Jordan Gibbons sat drinking
Glengoyne whisky in a Kearvaig bothy.
A trip to the distillery was decided
upon and, given its location on the West
Highland Way, it seemed like too good
of an opportunity not to link up another
distillery, Ben Nevis, by bike. Glyn Teifi-
Jones, their intrepid mountain biking
pal, joined them for the three days. His
reward? Sharing a tent with Jordan.

CHASING THE NORWEIGAN MIDNIGHT SUN

→

ROUTE
NORTH TO NARVIK

LOCATION
NORWAY

ONE OF THE great things about cycle touring in Norway is the concept of *allemannsretten* or "everyman's right," which allows anyone to roam free on uncultivated land. This right also extends to camping—you can pop your tent anywhere within reason.

Despite (or more likely because of) that freedom, finding the perfect spot to pitch a tent at the end of the day became Tim Warin's obsession. Athlyn Cathcart-Keays would be ready to fall asleep just about anywhere, but he would not rest until they found paradise for the night. There would be detours down dirt tracks, clambering over boulders, traipsing through thick forests, or carrying laden bikes across streams to seek out the best spot. Even in a country where you can camp wherever you like, the feeling of waking up without another soul around is worth the extra effort.

The pair would fall asleep with light still streaming through the tent canvas. Even at their start point in Trondheim, there was still light in the sky after 11 p.m. Once they crossed into the Arctic Circle, the sun would not drop below the horizon at all.

Athlyn and Tim's route trended north from Trondheim, hugging the Norwegian coastline and snaking its way up and over mountain passes before dropping back down to deep fjords. Ferry rides linked islands, archipelagos, and peninsulas, providing occasional respite from pedaling. Sometimes the road would take the straight option via a tunnel blasting through the hillside. These were a mixed blessing. The tunnels had low visibility, freezing temperatures, truck traffic, and a cacophony of ventilation for kilometers, but it all felt like a price worth paying when the pair surfaced and saw the mountain they had avoided scaling.

It was as a result of a wrong turn and a long tunnel that they did not want to experience in the other direction that the pair found the Kystriksveien, the scenic coastal route. A recently paved road meandered around rocky peaks, connecting every island with sculptural suspension bridges. As they wound their way along the road, walls of trees and rock opened out onto vast blue lakes where little yellow and red cottages held fort on grassy outcrops, with only a rowboat and pulley connecting them to the rest of the world.

The trees were so still, the water so placid, and the mountains so towering. They stopped for a long break at the side of a fjord, sitting in silence while taking it all in. The water was →

so tranquil that they took turns skimming stones across it just to watch it ripple, listening to the echo of their voices bounce until they left the valley completely.

The rhythm of touring when you are at the mercy of a ferry timetable is a funny thing. Athlyn and Tim would wake up bright and early with the intention of clocking a good distance before lunch, only to wait two or three hours at a port—an odd experience when you could sometimes see the next stretch of road rising out of the fjord just a few kilometers across the water. But one look at the map for an alternative way around will have you waiting obediently.

After the 100 kilometers (62 miles) to the Lofoten archipelago, the clouds blew in and the riders faced the Nordic weather they had been trying not to think about for the whole trip. Rather than stare out at the endless views, their eyes became fixed to the ground, watching for big puddles and keeping the rain off their faces.

The end of a journey is often a strange, discombobulating experience. The singular goal of arrival, well, arrives, and it feels as though the mind takes a while to readjust. What do you do now? And so when the time came and the couple finally rolled into Narvik with a day and a half to spare, their arrival was less ceremonious than they had anticipated. They stood perplexed outside of a shopping center. Was this it? Had they reached their end point?

With one night left, they hiked up a nearby mountain. After laying out the tent, they sat and surveyed the landscape that had been theirs to explore for the past two weeks, realizing they had hardly made a dent. As the sun momentarily hid behind the peaks across the fjord, it created an orange glow that highlighted every bug and blossom in the air. As she got ready to zip up the tent one last time, Athlyn realized that this was the first time she stayed awake long enough to see the midnight sun in all its glory. ○

"FERRY RIDES LINKED ISLANDS, ARCHIPELAGOS, AND PENINSULAS, PROVIDING OCCASIONAL RESPITE FROM PEDALING."

CAMPFIRE COOKING IN LOFOTEN—THE BEST WAY TO SPEND A REST DAY. SUPERMARKETS WERE SPARSE, BUT FARM STALLS OFTEN LINED THE ROAD.

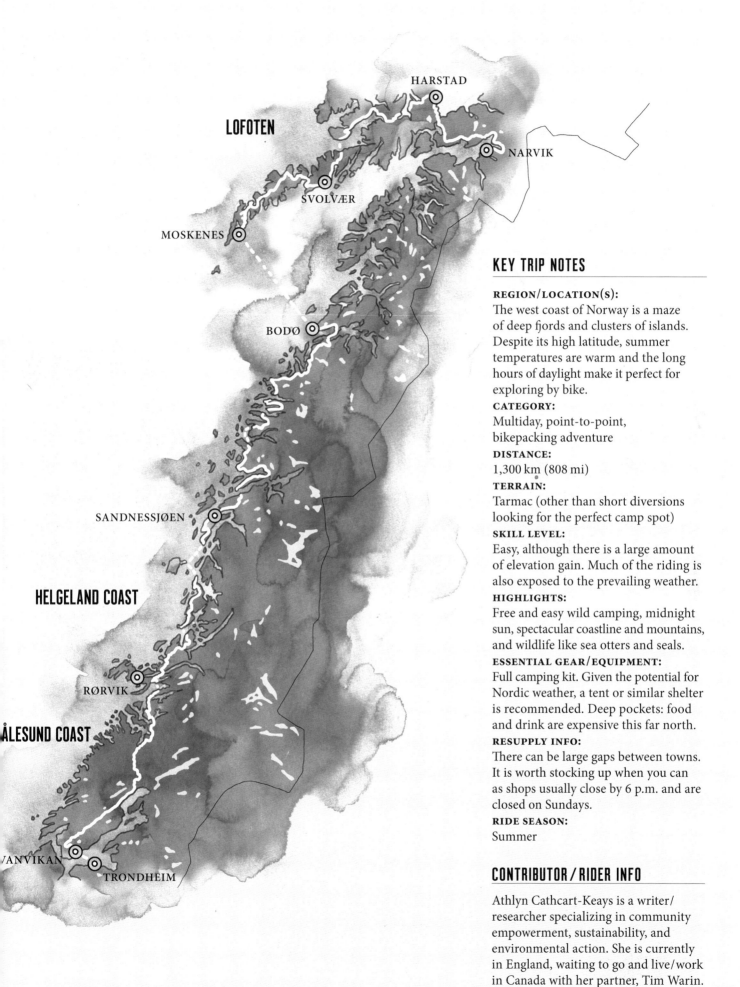

HARSTAD

LOFOTEN

NARVIK

SVOLVÆR

MOSKENES

BODØ

SANDNESSJØEN

HELGELAND COAST

RØRVIK

ÅLESUND COAST

VANVIKAN

TRONDHEIM

KEY TRIP NOTES

REGION/LOCATION(S):
The west coast of Norway is a maze
of deep fjords and clusters of islands.
Despite its high latitude, summer
temperatures are warm and the long
hours of daylight make it perfect for
exploring by bike.

CATEGORY:
Multiday, point-to-point,
bikepacking adventure

DISTANCE:
1,300 km (808 mi)

TERRAIN:
Tarmac (other than short diversions
looking for the perfect camp spot)

SKILL LEVEL:
Easy, although there is a large amount
of elevation gain. Much of the riding is
also exposed to the prevailing weather.

HIGHLIGHTS:
Free and easy wild camping, midnight
sun, spectacular coastline and mountains,
and wildlife like sea otters and seals.

ESSENTIAL GEAR/EQUIPMENT:
Full camping kit. Given the potential for
Nordic weather, a tent or similar shelter
is recommended. Deep pockets: food
and drink are expensive this far north.

RESUPPLY INFO:
There can be large gaps between towns.
It is worth stocking up when you can
as shops usually close by 6 p.m. and are
closed on Sundays.

RIDE SEASON:
Summer

CONTRIBUTOR/RIDER INFO

Athlyn Cathcart-Keays is a writer/
researcher specializing in community
empowerment, sustainability, and
environmental action. She is currently
in England, waiting to go and live/work
in Canada with her partner, Tim Warin.

TEAMWORK AND CAMARADERIE ON THE SMOKE 'N' FIRE 400

→

ROUTE
IDAHO SMOKE 'N' FIRE 400

LOCATION
UNITED STATES

ANDRÉ KAJLICH shuffled up the long single-track climb away from Galena, Illinois, toward Titus Lake in Idaho. He threw his fists forward, buried them into the dirt, and dragged his twin stumps forward before sitting down and repeating the process. Behind him, fellow members of the Challenged Athletes Foundation (CAF) took turns shuttling their bikes and André's hand tricycle up the trail, their headlamps twinkling in the dark as they made slow but steady progress. It was 11 p.m. and the group was almost halfway around the Smoke 'n' Fire 400 bike race. The 670-kilometer (421-mile) self-supported race starts and finishes in Boise, Idaho, and is described as "not for the faint hearted."

André is anything but faint hearted. After a night out with friends while studying in Prague, he was struck by a subway train. He lost his left leg at the hip and his right leg above the knee. That was nearly 20 years

ago, and since then he has competed in ultra-endurance events around the world. He prides himself in being able to keep up with able-bodied athletes, turning the cranks of his hand-powered mountain trike in a rowing-like motion. Now though, the loose terrain and narrow single-track of the Titus Lake climb made it impassable. The self-supported ethos of the Smoke 'n' Fire 400 forbids outside assistance. However, there is nothing to stop fellow racers from helping each other. "One-Armed Willie" Stewart, Mohamed Lahna (who has a single leg amputation due to a pelvis, hip, and femur disorder), Lucas Onan (riding with an underdeveloped left arm due to arthrogryposis), and veterans Mark Andrews and Anthony Skeesick worked together for 5 kilometers (two and a half miles) to reach the summit of the climb.

The team stuck together, moving as one. Each

person had their highs and lows, moments they were the strongest and times they needed support from the others. There were times they could ride side-by-side on long Forest Service dirt roads, sharing stories and jokes as they pedaled. Elsewhere, they would stop and regroup regularly, swapping snacks between each other. Mohamed pedaled with one leg, carrying a prosthetic limb strapped to his saddlebag ready to be fitted when the trail necessitated walking for a while. André would lean into the mountain on twisting off-camber singletrack descents, battling the inevitable toppling over as one wheel of his trike dropped off the edge of the trail. They did not always move quickly, but they sure as hell kept moving.

In the end, André and Mohamed had to pull out: the terrain and its impact on their bodies was too hard to endure. Was their teamwork at Titus Lake for nothing? Reflecting after the event, André was philosophical. →

ANDRÉ PILOTED HIS TRUSTY HAND TRICYCLE ALONG THE ROUTE.

One thing that life has taught him is not to be afraid to fail. He would rather enter an event that will push him to his limits than pick something safer and easier. Of course, it sucks to not complete any race, but he and the rest of the team got so much out of it.

The team had worked as a unit, supporting each other's goals over any single person's ambition. They achieved the apparently impossible during the course of a single sleep-deprived night and proved that teamwork trumps any obstacle. While not everyone completed the event, they far from failed. They all succeeded in proving that physical impairment is no barrier to epic feats of endurance. ○

ANDRÉ AND FELLOW CAF RIDER MOHAMED PUSHED THEIR BODIES TO THE LIMIT DURING THE EVENT.

THE RIDERS OF THE CHALLENGED ATHLETES FOUNDATION FREQUENTLY PROVE THAT PHYSICAL IMPAIRMENT IS NO BARRIER TO EPIC FEATS.

KEY TRIP NOTES

REGION/LOCATION(S):
Idaho

CATEGORY:
Bikepacking race,
epic challenge

DISTANCE:
670 km (421 mi)

TERRAIN:
Doubletrack, big gravel and
dirt Forest Service roads,
challenging singletrack,
some hike-a-bike, and a few
paved roads.

SKILL LEVEL:
Advanced. The route has been
ridden in as little as a day and
a half, but it is recommended
to aim for closer to five to six
days for a more leisurely pace.

HIGHLIGHTS:
Hot dips in geothermal
springs, scenic mountain
ranges, and friendly towns.

**ESSENTIAL GEAR/
EQUIPMENT:**
Mountain bike, camp gear,
GPS device, and bear spray,
since the route passes
through bear country.

RESUPPLY INFO:
Good resupply options
along the route, particularly
in Stanley, Ketchum, and
Featherville. Water is plentiful
en route. Note that some of
the smaller stores are not
always guaranteed to be open.

RIDE SEASON:
The race takes place in
September each year. The
route is best tackled between
July and September.

CONTRIBUTOR/RIDER INFO

The team included four
athletes from the Challenged
Athletes Foundation—André
Kajlich, Willie Stewart, Lucas
Onan, and Mohamed Lahna—
alongside two members of the
veterans charity Mission43,
Mark Andrews and Anthony
Skeesick. The group was
riding to raise money for CAF.

A ROUTE FOR STRONG NERVES

→

ROUTE
TAHOE TWIRL

LOCATION
UNITED STATES

"Is it called bikepacking because it is like backpacking, but instead of carrying your backpack, you carry your bike?" muttered Ryan Van Duzer, partly to himself, partly to his camera as he documented his and ride partner Dom Gill's circumnavigation around Lake Tahoe. They were most of the way through their third day on the trail and near their most southerly point, close to the state border between California and Nevada. The climbing was beginning to take its toll: we all have those moments and they always pass, usually as soon as the trail begins to point in the other direction. Fortunately, the crest of the climb was not far away.

The pair giggled and hollered as they railed down a perfect singletrack. The smooth snake of trail was interspersed with occasional drop-offs and hairpins requiring concentration. Tired bodies were matched with wired minds and tickles of adrenaline (and possibly caffeine, thanks to Dom's questionable energy-gel-in-a-corn-tortilla trail snack), keeping them on their toes until the route spat them out at Star Lake. It had been their goal for the entire day, a location that had stood out in the weeks beforehand when they pored over the map. "We have to camp there!" they exclaimed.

Rocky peaks plummeted straight into the far shores of the lake, snow patches tucked into north-facing gullies. The low sun backlit the summits and projected mountain-shaped shadows onto this most perfect of campsites. Dom and Ryan quickly erected their tent, before stripping down and charging into the bracing water. Storm clouds bubbled up behind the peaks above them, threatening a deluge that never came. The clouds dissipated as quickly as they appeared, as the sun fully dipped below the mountaintops and a full array of stars lit the night sky. Their tent glowed like a tiny firefly in the great expanse. It was the kind of location that feeds the soul. While there was beauty to be found all along the remarkably diverse landscapes surrounding Lake Tahoe, this was special, made even more so by the effort required to reach it.

The start of the pair's ride in Truckee, California, felt a long time ago. The high mountains that surrounded them now were a far cry from the lakeside singletrack where they used to tick off fun kilometers with fresh legs. That first ribbon of trail had given way to wide gravel tracks as they climbed through pastoral alpine landscapes and then descended down desert jeep tracks to Reno, Nevada, where they spent their first night in a hotel.

There are upsides and downsides to starting a long day in a town. The upside is the opportunity to fuel up with an all American big breakfast. The downside is the lethargic first few miles while your body works double-time to digest everything. After a few kilometers of flat tarmac, the pair began climbing. It was long and arduous, but with each meter gained they left behind the oven-like heat of Reno and eventually re-entered the alpine-like peaks. They paused briefly to dunk their heads in the first stream they forded, rinsing caked salt from their cheeks. And then they kept climbing, for the rest of the day, to a first night under the stars and striking distance from Star Lake.

Much of their third day utilized the Tahoe Rim Trail. The classic hiking loop of Lake Tahoe only has sections that are open to bikes, but the legal trails were glorious. Dom's and Ryan's tires barely left the singletrack as they rode through woods, crossed high passes, completed their hike-a-bike, and finally reached the location that inspired them so much: the ultimate camp location.

The trip was far from over—there was a long day ahead of them tomorrow—but in many ways, they felt complete. While the practicalities of the ride meant there was a route to follow, the goal of the trip was simply to get into the mountains for a few days and enjoy some truly great riding. So, drifting off to sleep, it was already mission accomplished. ○

EVERYTHING IS OK WHEN YOU
ARRIVE AT THE END OF A LONG
DAY AT AN ALPINE LAKE TO
JUMP INTO, ESPECIALLY WHEN
IT'S STAR LAKE, NEVADA.

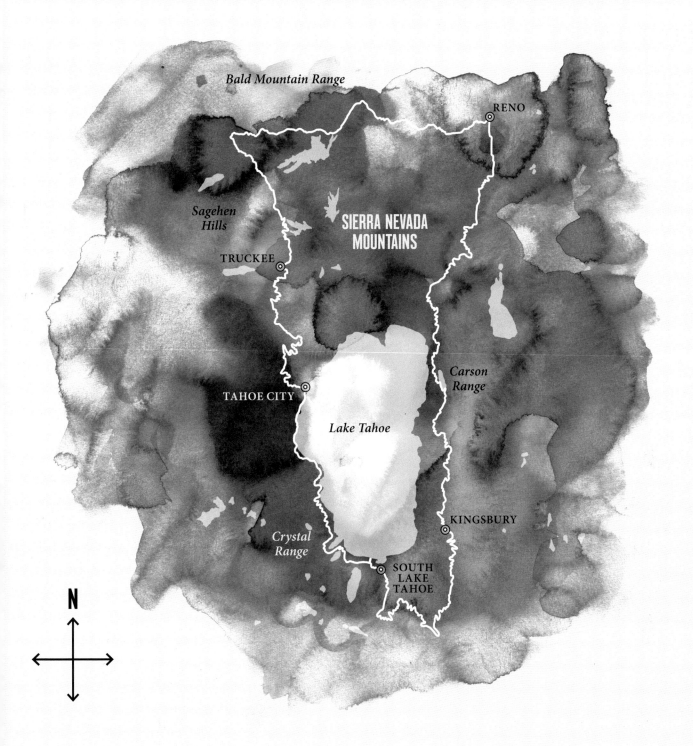

Bald Mountain Range

RENO

Sagehen
Hills

SIERRA NEVADA
MOUNTAINS

TRUCKEE

Carson
Range

TAHOE CITY

Lake Tahoe

Crystal
Range

KINGSBURY

SOUTH
LAKE
TAHOE

N

KEY TRIP NOTES

REGION/LOCATION(S):
Lake Tahoe straddles California
and Nevada, nestled in the
Sierra Nevada mountains.

CATEGORY:
Circular loop, singletrack shredding
mountain bike loop

DISTANCE:
300 km (186 mi). Four to five
days allows time for swim breaks
and relaxed evenings.

TERRAIN:
Mellow singletrack and gravel roads. Some
more technical and/or exposed sections.

SKILL LEVEL:
Advanced. While the trail can be ridden
at a mellow pace, there is 6,000 meters
(19,685 feet) of climbing/descending
on the route. A good level of fitness
and mountain bike skills will make
the experience much more enjoyable.

HIGHLIGHTS:
Epic flowing singletrack descents
and perfect camp spots.

ESSENTIAL GEAR/EQUIPMENT:
Mountain bike, camp kit, bug spray,
clothing to cope with cold nights and
hot days, two to three water bottles,
and a water filter. Be prepared
for occasional afternoon storms.

RESUPPLY INFO:
There are plenty of chances to resupply
each day. Larger supermarkets are
available in South Lake Tahoe, Tahoe
City, and Truckee.

RIDE SEASON:
Summer

CONTRIBUTOR/RIDER INFO

Dom Gill is a British award-winning
author, director, cinematographer, and
"outdoorphyllic." He lives on the banks
of Lake Tahoe. Ryan Van Duzer is a
runner, rider, and filmmaker. He lives
in Colorado.

TALES ON TYRES: TRANSPROVENCE

→

ROUTE
**GRANDE TRAVERSÉE
L'ALPES-PROVENCE**

LOCATION
FRANCE

THE ROAD CLIMB out of Barcelonnette changed into a narrow dirt track and quickly petered out into a smooth singletrack trail. The grins on Franziska Wernsing's and Jona Riechmann's faces grew wider as they followed the changing surface. The pair dashed through shimmering larch forests and pedaled into an expansive alpine meadow. The trail down was rocky, technical, and engaging riding, but as fun as it was difficult to negotiate on a loaded bike. When they finally rolled out their sleeping pads that night, they could not sleep. They still felt high on the day's riding, brimming with excitement about what was still to come. After passing through the mountains of the Provence Alps the year before, the pair knew a little of what to expect, but could not wait to see more.

Think of Provence and you are more likely to picture lavender fields and the Côte d'Azur than you are mountainous terrain, but the north of the region is crowded with tightly packed contours, hilltop villages, and a maze of trails connecting them. Franzi and Jona grew used to the saw-toothed profile of the route. Idyllic high alpine pastures sat above pine forests and steep-sided valleys.

Up high, remote shepherds' huts were nestled into cliffs. Sometimes a large sheepdog would raise its head as the pair passed, before returning to dozing in the midday sun once it decided they were no threat to his flock. The descents continued to be challenging, absorbing affairs that were even harder when the riders' eyes were drawn to new landscapes opening out in front of them. At times all they could do was pause, regather, and take in the sights.

Most of the time, the two riders met no one else on the trail. Their human interactions were often limited to ordering pâtisseries as they drooled over fruit tarts, *pain au chocolat* →

89

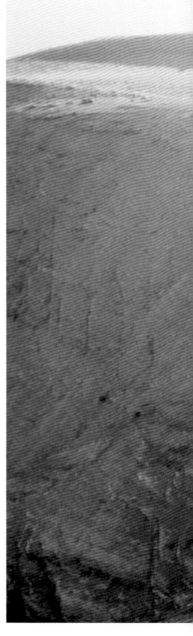

and savory quiches, their hunger only tempered by the limited space in their frame bags. One evening though, as the sun tickled the mountaintops on its descent toward darkness, Franzi and Jona met two elderly women hiking down the trail. They exchanged pleasantries before learning that the locals had made a wrong turn somewhere and were now too far away to make it home in daylight. They walked as foursome for the 10 kilometers (6 miles) to the nearest road, the riders' lights guiding them down the trail, with the Milky Way streaked across the sky above them. A few hours later they reached the remote road and the women were met by a friend, eternally thankful for the help that the two riders had provided. It was a moment of trail kindness that is paid forward and back; taking care of each other in the mountains is not a heroic act, rather just one of courtesy and decency.

Franzi and Jona trended southwest and as they did so, the landscape

subtly changed. Each valley had its own identity. The cooling winds of the high plateaus were replaced by increasingly hot hillsides and bleached-white rock. There were roller-coaster sections of trail carving their way through dark shale, with the occasional wildflower or tree poking through.

As the pair closed in on their destination of Manosque, the air popped with herbal lavender aromas as they brushed past wild bushes on the side of the trail. It was a sign that their time in the Alpes de Provence was coming to a close, but the pair made a note to return once again. There was still so much to discover. ○

EXPOSED SINGLE-TRACK IN THE HIGH MOUNTAINS: THERE'S MUCH MORE TO PROVENCE THAN LAVENDER FIELDS.

REFUELING WAS VITAL
ON A ROUTE WITH SO
MUCH HIKE-A-BIKE,
ESPECIALLY WHEN THE
LOCAL DELICACIES
TASTED SO GOOD.

KEY TRIP NOTES

REGION/LOCATION(S):
Alpes-de-Haute-Provence

CATEGORY:
Point-to-point mountain bike adventure

DISTANCE:
300 km (186 mi)

TERRAIN:
Gravel, technical mountain bike singletrack

SKILL LEVEL:
Advanced

HIGHLIGHTS:
Some of the best mountain biking trails in the world, endless supplies of pastries, and local delicacies in the villages en route.

ESSENTIAL GEAR/ EQUIPMENT:
Mountain bike, a waterproof layer for the frequent yet brief afternoon storms, and a map and GPS, although the trail is clearly signposted.

RESUPPLY INFO:
The route passes through towns and villages at regular intervals. Almost all have a local boulangerie/pâtisserie and small supermarket. Beware: hours can be variable and shops are often closed on Sundays. All villages will have at least one drinking-water tap in the village center.

RIDE SEASON:
Spring and autumn are ideal. Summer can be stiflingly hot, while much of the route is under snow and impassable during winter.

CONTRIBUTOR/RIDER INFO

Franziska Wernsing and Jona Riechmann are "Tales on Tyres." This trip was part of a longer six-month tour through Europe. The pair live for riding and exploring, and have undertaken numerous bikepacking trips, ranging from overnighters to longer explorations.

TRAILSIDE FIXES

Adventuring off-road in remote places by bike is tough on both bikepackers and equipment, not only because of challenging terrain but also the increased loads and harsh conditions. Here are the key kits, tools, spares, and fixes to know and carry to keep you and your bike on track.

CHECKLIST OF COMMON FIXES

While it is easy to ignore the fact things might go wrong, the side of a remote track in a storm is not the best place to start learning how to fix the basics. Before you leave, have a mechanic check your bike over.

The most likely parts to need maintenance during a bikepacking adventure will be those that are used the most, vulnerable, or with moving parts. With the exception of a few major failures or breaks that require more specific tools and knowledge—such as hubs and hydraulics—most issues are fixable with a few basics that you should carry.

A *Fixing a Flat Tire—Tube/Tubeless*
1 / 3 / 4 / 6 / 14 / 17 / 22
B *Repairing a Split Tire*
1 / 3 / 5 / 16 / 32
C *Installing/Removing Pedals*
2

D *Adjusting Brakes/Replacing Brake Pads*
2 / 11 / 23
E *Adjusting Gears—Cable Tensions/Derailleur Alignments*
2 / 11
F *Fixing/Replacing a Chain*
7 / 10 / 11 / 18 / 19
G *Adjusting Handlebars/Stems/Headsets/Saddle/Seatpost*
2
H *Replacing Cables*
2 / 11 / 12 / 27

TOOLS GRID

ESSENTIAL: 1 *Pump.*
2 *Allen/hex keys.* 3 *Tire levers.* 4 *Patch kit.*
5 *Tire boot.* 6 *Tubeless plugs kit.* 7 *Chain breaker.*
8 *Zip ties.* 9 *Duct/electrical tape.* 10 *Rag.* 11 *Pliers.*
12 *Cutters.*
EXPEDITION: 13 *Spoke key.*
14 *Valve extractor.* 15 *Super glue.* 16 *Needle and thread.*
Multi-tools have various separate tools like chain breakers, tubeless plugs, and pliers integrated on them, so check how you can efficiently carry less.

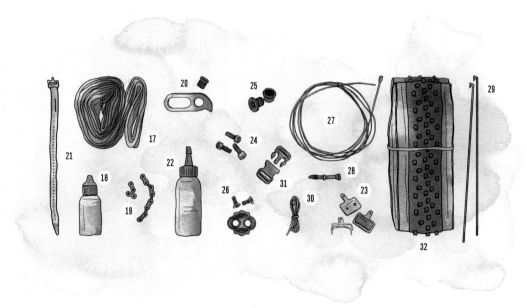

SPARES GRID

ESSENTIAL: 17 *Inner tubes (check sizing).* 18 *Chain lube.*
19 *Chain section and quick links (check compatibility).*
20 *Derailleur/mech hanger (check compatibility).*
21 *Bungee/strap.*
EXPEDITION: 22 *30–50 ml tubeless sealant.* 23 *Brake pads (check compatibility)*
24 *Bolts (M4/M5).* 25 *Chain-ring nuts and bolts.* 26 *Cleat and cleat bolts.* 27 *Brake/gear cables.* 28 *Valves.* 29 *Spokes (check lengths).* 30 *Guyline/lace.* 31 *Bag buckles.* 32 *Tire.*

FIRST AID GRID

33 *Plasters.* 34 *Bandage dressings.* 35 *Sterile wipes.*
36 *Steristrips.* 37 *Rubber gloves.* 38 *Hydrocortisone/ Sudocrem (for saddle sores).*
39 *Painkillers.*
40 *Antibiotics.*
41 *Dioralyte electrolyte sachets (for rehydration).*
42 *Diamox (for altitude).*
43 *Antihistamines (for allergies).* 44 *TCP antiseptic liquid.* 45 *Lip balm.* 46 *Tweezers/tick pullers.*
47 *Small scissors.*
48 *Emergency bivvy.*

SHELTER

The art of minimalism—balancing comfort, safety, and agility—comes with experience. Learning from your successes and mistakes is the best way to prepare for future adventures. These are the three main shelter options in the backcountry.

SEEKING A CAMP SPOT
- Flat and dry-ish
- Sheltered
- Away from roads, tracks, rockfall, animals, rivers, and steep drops
- Water supply for cooking, drinking, and washing bodies/sporks
- Pitch up just before dark to check surroundings and not attract attention

WILD CAMPING/LEAVE NO TRACE
- Research terrain and legalities
- Ask for permission
- Camp on durable surfaces
- Pack all trash out with you
- Cathole human waste
- Minimize campfire impact
- Respect animals and plants

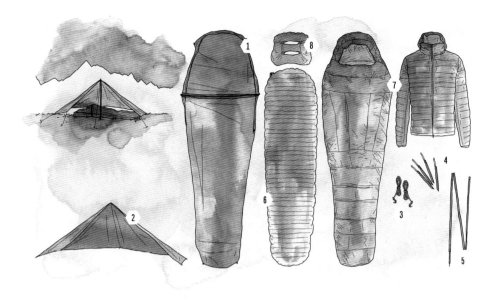

BIVVY / TARP

Quick, simple, lightweight, but exposed. Tarps add fuss but provide additional shelter.

1 *Bivvy Bag*
2 *Tarp*
3 *Guylines*
4 *Pegs*
5 *Pole(s)*
6 *Sleeping mat*
7 *Sleeping bag/insulated jacket*
8 *Pillow*

TOP TIP: Leave your system together and roll up for a simple roll out in the evening.

TENT

The go-to. Your home away from home.

1 *Tent inner/outer*
2 *Additional groundsheet*
3 *Poles*
4 *Guylines*
5 *Pegs*
6 *Sleeping mat*
7 *Sleeping bag*
8 *Pillow*

TOP TIP: Do not view a tent as a single item. Think about splitting up the various pieces to aid packability. (inner/outer in handlebar pack; poles/pegs in frame pack, etc.)

HUT

It offers less freedom than camping out, but the joy of reaching a pass-nesting mountain hut or remote stone bothy is unrivaled. Huts are a great introduction to bikepacking and mean carrying less kit.

1 *Sleeping mat*
2 *Sleeping bag*
3 *Sleeping bag liner*
4 *Pillow*

TOP TIP: Phone ahead to make sure the mountain huts are open and have space, and to give them a rough arrival time. Bring earplugs.

SUSTENANCE

*Whether roughing it and surviving on pouched meals or cozy camping
and gourmet cooking, fueling is fundamental for avoiding a bikepacking disaster.
Here are some considerations for eating and drinking in the wild.*

WATER TIPS

● Add cordial, fresh citrus slices, or electrolyte sachets (in moderation) to liven water up.

● Filter, purify, or boil all surface water unless direct from a spring or high enough not to be contaminated.

Collect from flowing sources and avoid stagnant water.

FOOD TIPS

● Wet or dry food? Dehydrated pouch meals are convenient, packable, good for dense calories. They keep fresh for longer but do require water.

● Gas canister stoves are most popular for packability and efficiency. Multi-fuel stoves are a better option for longer, remote trips as they can burn on any widely available liquid fuels.

ULTRALIGHT COOKING

Quick, simple, and lightweight, but limited for cooking proper meals. See it more as boiling water for dehydrated pouch meals, dried foods like noodles/pastas, and hot drinks.

1 *Stove: canister/alcohol*
2 *Small pot*
3 *Fuel/lighter*
4 *Windshield*
5 *Spork*
6 *Food supplies*
7 *Water*

TOP TIP: Boil directly in and eat out of your single-wall camping mug.

GOURMET COOKING

Keeping it to one-pot meals will make preparation, cooking, and cleaning up easier and quicker.

1 *Stove: canister/multi-fuel*
2 *Pot(s)/kettle*
3 *Fuel/lighter*
4 *Windshield*
5 *Knife and spork*
6 *Food supplies*
7 *Water*
8 *Herbs/spices*
9 *Garnish grater*

TOP TIP: Decant herbs/spices, pastes/sauces, and/or stock cubes into smaller reusable pots or bottles.

DRINKING

The essentials (clean water for drinking) and the nice-to-haves (prepping and brewing hot drinks).

1 *Water containers: bottles/bladder*
2 *Water filter: hand/in-line*
3 *Purification tabs*
4 *Mug*
5 *Instant sachets*
6 *Coffee/tea supplies*
7 *Collapsible dripper*
8 *Aeropress Go*
9 *Moka pot*
10 *Tea ball*

TOP TIP: Bladders are a good way of carrying larger volumes of water.

RIDING THE BADGER FROM INVERNESS TO GLASGOW

→

ROUTE
BADGER DIVIDE

LOCATION
SCOTLAND

"GENERAL WADE was a bastard," exclaimed Tom Hill part way up the loose gravel track that makes up the northern side of the Corrieyairack Pass. Tom and the group had been lured into a false sense of security after the relatively easy first 50 kilometers (31 miles) of the Great Glen Way, an undulating trail carrying them out of the relative metropolis of Inverness to the historic town of Fort Augustus.

Knowing they were about to hit the most remote section of the route, the group stocked up on essentials—like three varieties of the Scottish confectionery Tunnock's—at a gas station mini market. As an afterthought, a couple of the wise members of the team shoved some packets of couscous and oatcakes into the shopping basket.

The Corrieyairack Pass was built in the mid-1700s. It was part of a wide network of military roads commissioned by General George Wade (he of bastard infamy) to help him move British troops around more efficiently and keep the pesky Jacobite Scots

under control. That was all well and good, ignoring the brutal exertion of control over the local population. Except Wade did seem to purposefully choose some brutal climbs for his roads. It might have been nicer if he had popped in a chairlift or something as well. Ah well, onwards and upwards. And upwards a bit more. To be fair to Wade, despite being 300 years old, the road was holding up pretty well. The surface was loose enough that it was necessary to stay seated while winching up in the lowest gear available, but it was always (just) rideable. The group climbed away in pitches, pausing and regathering.

It was during one of those stops that the first wave of rain swept through and sent the riders rushing to pull their waterproof gear on. Tom tugged at his saddle pack, accidentally sending his not-so-carefully stashed chocolate supplies flying in a panicked attempt to find his dry layer deep inside the luggage. Amateur hour—and he was meant to be the experienced one.

Suitably protected from the weather, it →

seemed rude not to have a snack before carrying on, seeing as there was a long way to go and all. They weren't yet 100 kilometers (62 miles) to the Badger Divide. What is the Badger? Well, it is not a single trail. You will not find signposts for it, or a line on the map. It is the invention of a Scottish rider named Stu Allan. He decided to use existing long-distance routes like the Great Glen Way to link the cities of Inverness and Glasgow. The result is a route that takes in the most remote parts of the Scottish Highlands on terrain that is mostly smooth enough to make gravel bikes the ideal choice.

Speaking of which, not all gravel is the same. Decked in their waterproof layers, the gang crested the summit of the pass and continued their journey south. Just as the ascent was challenging, the descent was equally as bad. Loose rocks the size of fists rolled under skinny tires as the group bounced their way down the switchback turns, blinking rain and grit out of their eyes as they rode. Ahead lay the majestic Loch Laggan, another long climb to the "highest train station in the U. K." at Corrour,

and crossing the bleak yet beautiful Rannoch Moor. For now though, as the rain got heavier still, the small bothy at the side caught their eye. It may have been a bit early, but the promise of a fire and a dry night under a roof was too tempting to pass by.

Oh, one last thing. Why is the route called the Badger Divide? Well, it takes its name from a mispronunciation of the Mexican Baja Divide, which is best said in a thick Scottish accent. What the Badger lacks in deserts it makes up for in some of the best gravel adventures that Scotland has to offer. And Tunnock's. ○

"GENERAL WADE WAS A
BASTARD," WE MUTTER
REPEATEDLY AS WE CLIMB
THE CORRIEYAIRACK PASS,
RIDING THROUGH HISTORY.

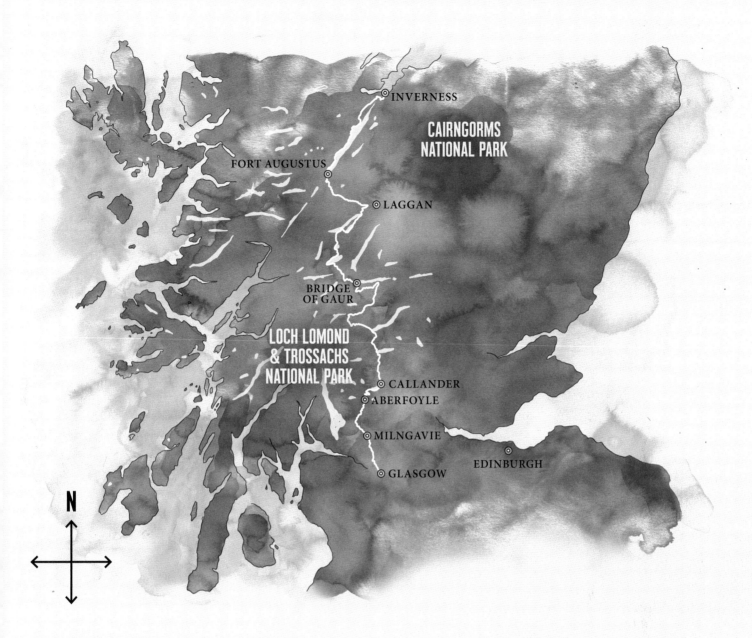

INVERNESS

CAIRNGORMS
NATIONAL PARK

FORT AUGUSTUS

LAGGAN

BRIDGE
OF GAUR

LOCH LOMOND
& TROSSACHS
NATIONAL PARK

CALLANDER
ABERFOYLE

MILNGAVIE

GLASGOW   EDINBURGH

N

KEY TRIP NOTES

REGION/LOCATION(S):
The Badger Divide runs from
Inverness to Glasgow, through the
Scottish Highlands and Trossachs.

CATEGORY:
Point-to-point bikepacking, long
weekender

DISTANCE:
320 km (199 mi). Allow 3–5 days to
enjoy the ride and views along the way.

TERRAIN:
Mixed terrain. Everything from
gravel to rocky trails, to buff
singletrack. The majority of the
riding is on good-quality gravel.

SKILL LEVEL:
Intermediate. The route terrain is
technically straightforward. There is
over 5,000 meters (16,404 feet) of
climb along the length of the route,
so a reasonable level of fitness is

required. Some of the route is
extremely remote, so riders should be
prepared for and comfortable dealing
with potential mechanical issues.

HIGHLIGHTS:
A different perspective on Scotland
for even the most seasoned visitor to
the country. The small, picturesque
Corrour train station is literally in the
middle of nowhere, surrounded by
remote peaks.

ESSENTIAL GEAR/EQUIPMENT:
Camp kit, sleeping shelter (unless
you get very lucky, you are unlikely to
experience no rain at all during your
ride), layers of clothing to cope with
all conditions, Tunnock's teacakes,
and midge net and repellant if riding
between May and September.

RESUPPLY INFO:
Resupply points are very limited at
certain points on the ride. Make sure
you leave Fort Augustus with

enough supplies for the next couple
of days riding. The train station cafe
at Corrour serves food but can be
fully booked. The next major resupply
point is not until Killin, 235 km
(140 mi) in.

RIDE SEASON:
Can be ridden all year round, but
most pleasant in spring and autumn.
The route may be impassable in
places due to snow in winter.
During the summer, a breezy camp
spot will help to naturally avoid
the worst of the midges.

CONTRIBUTOR/RIDER INFO

Tom Hill is a writer based in Bradford,
England. He has completed many trips
with photographer Sam Needham.
They were joined on the Badger Divide
by Oliver Moore, Julia Hobson, and
Rachael Walker.

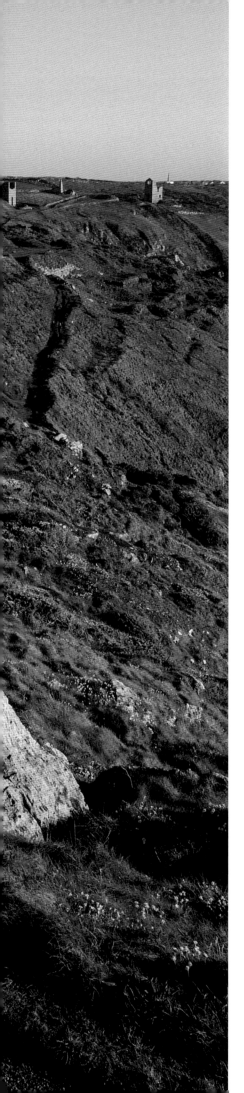

DISCOVERING SOUTHWEST CORNWALL AND ITS FOOD REVOLUTION

→

ROUTE
CULINARY CORNWALL

LOCATION
ENGLAND

CORNWALL's 700-kilometer (435-mile) coastline and lush rolling lands make the peninsula a prolific natural larder boasting the very best quality seafood, meat, dairy products, crops, and wild food. With these world-class ingredients making their way into the hands of food makers, food entrepreneurs, and chefs, it is no surprise that Cornwall is a renowned foodie destination. The county is promoted and led by celebrity chefs who are generating a wave of popularity for Cornish produce and eateries, at a time when food provenance is high on the agenda. Time to book return trains to Penzance to find out more about the coast, land, eateries, and wild produce.

Newlyn's harborside would've bustled as the boats docked with their catches just a few hours before Harry Engels, Danny Janes, and Stefan parked up for a Jelbert's ice cream. Even then, in the calm after the storm, forklifts were busy dumping used ice into the harbor waters, and the flocks of seagulls squawked frantically over their pickings.

With the evening's seafood— whole mackerel and scallops—sourced and strapped safely to bikes, Harry, Danny, and Stefan pedaled further west for a clifftop coastal cookout. Riding up out of Mousehole, one of the many quaint Cornish villages whose harbor wall shelters a fleet of small fishing boats, the concept of the "Cornish mile" hits home. It is a much longer and steeper version of a traditional mile, as the roads track the relentless rolling hills and jagged coastlines. Passing the Minack Theatre, Land's End, and the remains of the Botallack tin mines in the lowering sun, a spot on the cliff tops was needed. Do not expect to get down to the sea on a whim around here. Having slowly collected kindling and small firewood over the course of the day, a small fire was lit and seafood prepped by gutting and washing the mackerels and seasoning them with lemon, the amazing pepper by Cornish Sea Salt, and lots of parsley, before cooking them in foil on the hot embers. As the foilbubbled away, sea crashed below, and sun finally set over the Celtic Sea's horizon, →

FORAGING WITH LOCALS.
CORNWALL BOASTS A
FINE NATURAL, COASTAL
LARDER. THAT'S A BASKET
OF WILD SAMPHIRE.

"SINGLETRACK ROADS, GREAT PLACES TO STAY, GREAT FOOD, AND THE ODD FERRY-HOP, WHAT MORE COULD YOU WANT FROM A BIKE TRIP?"

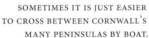

SOMETIMES IT IS JUST EASIER TO CROSS BETWEEN CORNWALL'S MANY PENINSULAS BY BOAT.

sporks were readied. There is no doubt that Cornish mackerel tastes even better cooked up on Cornish cliffs.

Riding onwards from Sennen, expect one of the finest stretches of touring road in the United Kingdom, winding through coastal farms and moorlands to St Ives, saffron buns, hedge-lined roads (hedgerows are a time-honored way for farmers to break the prevailing westerly winds that blow off the sea), farm shops, Cornish pasties (a staple among the mine workers who made them popular in the nineteenth century), ferry-hops, Cornish Yarg cheese starters, steaks, Cornish blue cheese, hidden beachfront huts, Falmouth delicatessens and coffee shops, oyster estuaries, mussel pots, more ferry-hops, more Cornish miles, and the Lizard Light-house. With local experts, shoreline seaweed, wild spinach, sea beet,

samphire, and lemony sorrell can all be foraged for.

From a first evening cooking deliciously simple mackerel over a cliff top open fire to a morning picking and munching wild samphire from the coastal grasslands, it is easy to see how established the Cornish food scene is where the very best locally sourced and foraged ingredients meet talented chefs and friendly food entrepreneurs in the most unique locations. But it is not just food. There is also an ace bikepacking network supporting it. With quiet, often singletrack roads, great places to stay, great food, and the odd ferry-hop, what more could you want from a bike trip? Load your bikes with cooking and camping gear, and bikepack Cornwall to discover the many producers and eateries for yourself. Harry, Danny, and Stefan merely scratched the surface. ○

AS WELL AS SOURCING
INGREDIENTS TO COOK
YOURSELF, PIT STOPS AT
THE VAST NETWORK OF
AMAZING EATERIES MAKE
FOR A REAL BIKEPACKER'S
TREAT—REWARDS
FOR THE CHALLENGING
COASTAL HILL RIDING.

"WITH THESE WORLD-CLASS INGREDIENTS IT IS NO SURPRISE THAT CORNWALL IS A RENOWNED FOODIE DESTINATION."

KEY TRIP NOTES

REGION/LOCATION(S):
Cornwall

CATEGORY:
2–3 day escape

DISTANCE:
200 km (125 mi)

TERRAIN:
Road

SKILL LEVEL:
Easy–intermediate

HIGHLIGHTS:
Sourcing, cooking, and
eating Cornish food outside,
ferry-hopping, and foraging.

**ESSENTIAL GEAR/
EQUIPMENT:**
Spork and camp cooking
kit, beach swimming kit,
and a mega appetite.

RESUPPLY INFO:
Penzance, St Ives, Truro,
St Mawes, Falmouth,
and all the eateries and
stores in-between. You will
not go hungry or thirsty
in Cornwall.

RIDE SEASON:
Year-round, but during May
to October to catch the
eateries open and in-season

CONTRIBUTOR/RIDER INFO

Culinary Cornwall was
a Pannier.cc production
inspired by the Cornish food
revolution movement and the
*Great Cornish Food Book: A
Collection of Recipes, Tales and
Morsels from the Ocean, Fields
and Cliff Tops of Cornwall,*
which helped Stefan plot all
the producers and eateries.
Joining him on this trip
were pals Danny Janes and
Harry Engels (photographer),
neither of whom expected
to be carrying whole
mackerels on their bikes.

BEATING RISING SEA LEVELS ON THE WADDEN

→

ROUTE
WADDEN ISLANDS HOPPING

LOCATION
THE NETHERLANDS

THE GROUP RODE along never-ending, empty beaches. The sand was as white as the insides of their shorts tan lines. There were no towering boulevards with corny tourist shops, no frantic surf lineups, no labyrinth of beach towels to navigate, just infinite stretches of the finest sand marked by the faded greens of dune reeds and perfect painted skies.

There were a few remarkable things about this scene. Firstly, this was not a Caribbean island, but the Wadden Islands, located off the northern coast of the Netherlands. Secondly, the weather was amazing. This is not the case for some 315 days of the year, which could explain why the beaches were so empty. Finally, the Wadden Islands might not exist at all in a few years' time. We will return to that, but for now the only sense of distress was felt by the one group member—who will remain unnamed—who almost missed the first ferry. Fortunately, they got waved on board two minutes passed the departure time by a friendly boatman and a supportive crowd of co-passengers.

There is a lot to be said for Type II Fun, i. e. the kind of fun that is dismal in the moment but fun in retrospect. This trip wasn't about that though. It was firmly Type I on the fun scale: fun in the moment. Lian van Leeuwen and a group of friends boarded the ferry with plans for a long summer weekend over a three-day bikepacking trip across the beautiful islands that lie just off the coast of the Netherlands. The Wadden Sea, an area that stretches through the Netherlands, Germany, and Denmark, is on the UNESCO World Heritage list. It is the largest tidal flat system in the world, where natural processes proceed undisturbed, accommodating a rich bio-diversity of both aquatic and terrestrial species. The long, thin chain of the Wadden Islands is a truly unique place.

After the initial ferry hiccup, the group enjoyed three leisurely days of island hopping by bike at a pace solely determined by ferry schedules. There was little point in rushing as it would only lead to waiting later on. Their days were as full of beachside →

111

THE WADDEN ISLANDS WERE CREATED WHEN TIDAL ACTION SHAPED LARGE SAND DUNES INTO THE 500 KM (311 MI) LONG ARCHIPELAGO.

barbecues, local beers, and sans-Lycra dips in mellow ocean waves as they were easy trail rides.

Shoes filled up with sand and ocean spray marked bike bags with salt stains while they sailed on yet another small ferry. Silly inside jokes merged the group into a single-celled organism.

Threads of humor would stretch out over the entire weekend, punchlines growing funnier each time they were retold. There was always time to stop for a story, explore a small harbor, or take a dip in the sea.

And then the heat. Those three days of eternal summer turned out to be part of one of the most extreme heat waves Europe has ever experienced, with temperatures rising up to 45.9 degrees Celsius in France—the hottest June day ever recorded. It slowed the riders down in a wonderful way. It was impossible to hurry. Any effort above cruising pace was punished quickly. The self-generated breeze

WITH A RELAXED
SCHEDULE, THERE
WAS ALWAYS TIME FOR
SUNBATHING.

while cycling kept life bearable in all but the midday sun. For those times, an abundance of local beers and burgers helped. The group could not have asked for more.

While the heat brought easy living for a weekend, it could also mean the end of the Wadden Islands. To understand why is to understand the entire Dutch psyche. Twelve thousand years ago, during the last Ice Age, the sea level was 60 meters (197 feet) lower than it is today, and the Wadden Islands were part of the European mainland. As the climate warmed, what were once huge coastal sand dunes formed into islands, and on the mainland, the →

Dutch entered into a long battle with water management to protect the country from rising sea levels.

But here is the spoiler: the pride of the Dutch is the Delta Works, a series of dams and barriers built to protect the country from a maximum rise of 45 centimeters (18 inches). With the current global carbon dioxide emissions, Dutch sea levels are predicted to rise two to three meters (seven to ten feet) in the next 100 years. The nation might be able to engineer their way out of that threat when it comes to protecting the mainland, but more vulnerable areas like the Wadden will likely not be as fortunate.

Lian and the group did ride paradise for three glorious days. But it is a paradise that might be lost within the course of our generation if we do not lower our global carbon emissions to combat the climate crisis. If we love where we ride, let's act accordingly. ○

THE HUNT FOR A SHADED LUNCH SPOT WAS A SERIOUS BUSINESS AS THE MERCURY ROSE.

"AFTER THE INITIAL FERRY HICCUP, THE GROUP ENJOYED THREE LEISURELY DAYS OF ISLAND HOPPING BY BIKE."

KEY TRIP NOTES

REGION/LOCATION(S):
The Wadden Islands lie along
the coast of the Netherlands,
stretching north to Germany
and Denmark.

CATEGORY:
Gravel touring at relaxed
pace, long weekender

DISTANCE:
Around 375 km (233 mi)

TERRAIN:
Easy off-road sandy trails,
forest trails, gravel,
and tarmac.

SKILL LEVEL:
Easy. Flat and non-
technical terrain.

HIGHLIGHTS:
All the fun of the beach
and enjoying a slow pace
of life for a few days.

**ESSENTIAL GEAR/
EQUIPMENT:**
Camp gear and a
bike suitable for light
off-road riding.

RESUPPLY INFO:
Plenty of towns and
villages en route for
burger and beer stops.

RIDE SEASON:
Spring to early autumn.

CONTRIBUTOR/RIDER INFO

Lian van Leeuwen is a
professional photographer.
She is an accomplished
bikepacker in her own
right, as well as an official
photographer for events
like the Atlas Mountains
Race. As the founder of Shift
Cycling Culture, she aims for
a more sustainable cycling
industry—a goal supported
by photographer and Lian's
riding partner Jelle Mul.
They were joined on their
trip by Chris McClean,
Michiel Braak, Dennis Bruin,
and Thijs Al.

ONTHOFEN

LLGÄU

ZILLERTAL ALPS

INNSBRUCK

MAYRHOFEN

Pfitscherjoch

4

Tre Cime
di Lavaredo

EASTERN ALPS

DOLOMITES

BOLZANO

MISURINA

Mt.
Ortler

SULDEN

CORTINA
D'AMPEZZO

1C

ORMIO

3

VENETIAN ALPS

Mt. Grappa

Mt. Pasubio

2

BASSANO
DEL GRAPPA

SCHIO

VENICE

BIKEPACKING THE
EUROPEAN ALPS

1A–C *In the Tracks
of Alpinists, Bonatti Tour*
2 *Grappa Massif Hutpacking*
3 *Looping the Ortler*
4 *Innsbruck Hutpacking*
5 *Allgäu to Finale Ligure*

IN THE TRACKS OF ALPINISTS

→

ROUTE
BONATTI TOUR

LOCATION
ITALY

CURATING A bikepacking trip around a theme is a great way to find a focus when planning a route from scratch. A theme—be it an activity like wild swimming, an interest like food and drink, or a geographical challenge like a riding coast-to-coast—helps define a starting point to build from. Otherwise, your options are endless. For this trip, Jordan Gibbons and Stefan's idea was to plot what became a series of routes in northern Italy that followed the tracks of famous Italian alpinist Walter Bonatti, one of the greatest mountaineers and climbers of all time. The routes would go through the Bergamasque Alps (where he grew up), the Mont Blanc massif (where he called home and spent a lot of time climbing), and the Dolomites (where he made his first expeditions). Riding on loaded bikepacking bikes, Stefan, Jordan, and Dan Easton's journey would merely scratch the gravel surface of Bonatti's alpine playgrounds, but the tour was less about his climbing endeavors than the associated mountain life and experience of spending time among the peaks he climbed, and in the huts and small towns that dotted the landscapes around them. These are also the ideal locations for big mountain lovers—and intrepid cyclists looking to tackle challenging terrain beyond where the roads end.

After a long day of riding in the Bergamasque Alps, that moment of swapping your cycling shoes for a pair of mountain hut slippers is hard to

beat. It's even better when you slip on a pair of bright pink Crocs. After threading through derelict ski resorts on the steep climb up from the rolling alpine meadows of Oltre il Colle, where farmers worked hard scything and shepherding into the dusky hours, Stefan, Jordan, and Dan arrived late and beaten at Rifugio Capanna, which overlooks Monte Alben. This was one of a network of more than 700 Club Alpino Italiano huts—an integral part of mountain and mountaineering life. After the trio's late arrival, they were led straight into the alpine memorabilia-cluttered dining room by the host Attilio and his family for a hearty meal of cheesy tomato pasta, stewed meat, fruit tart, and beers. This is the highest point of the ride of Monte Alben— the peak which, according to Bonatti's book *The Mountains of My Life,* most triggered his imagination "thanks to its jagged limestone spires, which were often wreathed in mist." The next morning, the group would descend the Zambla Pass before joining the Seriana Valley bike path back to Vertova.

In the wake of the morning sun, bikes were repack around outside benches and a tray full of Attilio's fine *rifugio* coffees and breakfast snacks. As all good bikepacking trips should, the overnight ride finished with a swim in the Serio river on the outskirts of Vertova, where bronzed locals lounged on deck chairs. Vertova is the town where Bonatti lived and studied, and the place where

nature and its luring peaks inspired him to go outdoors.

At the foot of the Mont Blanc massif, Courmayeur, the town Bonatti called home for most of his life, and the connecting valley-pass track network are as ideal a mountain playground as they come. Riding into Val Ferret, the granite peaks tower above, plunging the valley bottom into shadow while the echoing sound of clanging cowbells provides a soundtrack to the ride and the hike along the Tour du Mont Blanc trails, toward the welcoming lights of the Rifugio Bonatti. Walter Bonatti never actually lived in the *rifugio,* but visited numerous times, and it was named after him out of appreciation for the climber. From the hut's terrace you can see incredible views of Grandes Jorasses and the Walker Spur buttresses, the peaks and routes blithely selected by Bonatti and his friends for their very first Alpine summer in 1949.

The next challenge is the taxing road climb up into Val Veny, the valley that grows into the tallest peaks in Europe. It is also the site of some of Bonatti's most infamous climbs, most notably his retreat to the Gamba hut after the Frêney tragedy of 1961, when his group got caught in a savage storm while climbing the 800-meter (2,624-foot) granite pillar on the flanks of Mont Blanc. Pedaling higher, the group reached even more stunning gravel tracks and switchbacks of the Tour →

A SERIES OF TOURS RIDING THE MONT BLANC MASSIF, BERGAMASQUE ALPS, AND DOLOMITES IN THE TRACKS OF WALTER BONATTI.

YOU WON'T STRUGGLE FOR
LOCAL FOOD AND DRINK
SPECIALTIES, OR SWIM OR BIVVY
SPOTS IN THE MOUNTAINS
OF NORTHERN ITALY.

"OTHERS MAY ~~CLIMB~~ [RIDE] YOUR ROUTE, BUT NO ONE ELSE CAN HAVE THE SAME EXPERIENCE. THAT REMAINS YOURS ALONE."

— WALTER BONATTI —

du Mont Blanc, culminating with a refreshing toast to Bonatti at the Rifugio Elisabetta, which is perched at the foot of the Aiguille des Glaciers peak and commands views back over the Peuterey peaks and Mont Blanc beyond. This is the haven of the glaciers, jagged pillars, and remote ridges you read about in Bonatti's book.

The Dolomites' Cortina d'Ampezzo, the perennial tourist town with several cable car options, gravel routes, and world famous passes to explore by bike, was the third and final Bonatti route hub. After stocking up on Ferrero snacks, the group rode the Faloria cable car into the heartland of the Dolomites, a UNESCO World Heritage Site. Known as the "pale mountains," the Dolomites contrasted the gigantic granite of Courmayeur. This overnight trip reaches one of the *rifugios* up around the Tre Cime di Lavaredo— the three huge vertical stone fingers that were "the 'last great problems' of the thirties until climbed in 1937, and then in winter 1953, by Bonatti." Unlike Bonatti, who arrived by train and walked and skied up with all his expedition kit, for bikers there is a special route along gravel mountain bike and ski service tracks that joins the Tre Croci pass and eventually climbs the stunning Tre Cime pass up to the jagged limestone moonscape. Given the Dolomites' reputation as a climbing mecca, bikepackers share the Lavaredo mountain huts with climbers and hikers alike. The group spent the evening under the starlight, socializing and even sharing a negroni mixed at the bottom of the mountain, carried up, and garnished with fresh orange.

Early the next morning, Stefan, Jordan, and Dan packed their bikes for the last time alongside climbers filling their packs and checking all their ropes and gear for tackling the surrounding routes. A week of chasing the tracks of Walter Bonatti made for a great escape on the bikes. As Bonatti said, "mountaineering is only one of a thousand ways of living and getting to know yourself … it should never be mere escapism, because sooner or later we must return to our own personalities … the mountains should prepare us to go further."

Which of your heroes could you base a trip around? ○

THE UNESCO WORLD HERITAGE JAGGED PEAKS AND TRACKS OF THE DOLOMITES PROVIDE BIKEPACKERS WITH A SPECTACULAR PLAYGROUND.

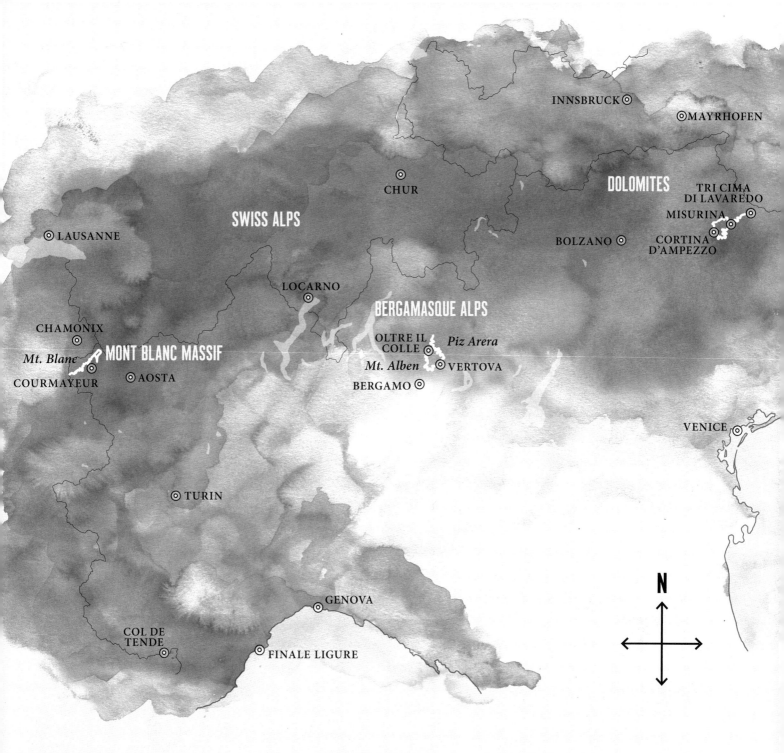

INNSBRUCK ◉

◉ MAYRHOFEN

CHUR ◉

SWISS ALPS

DOLOMITES

TRI CIMA
DI LAVAREDO

MISURINA

◉ LAUSANNE

BOLZANO ◉

CORTINA
D'AMPEZZO

LOCARNO
◉

BERGAMASQUE ALPS

CHAMONIX
◉

OLTRE IL
COLLE ◉

Piz Arera

MONT BLANC MASSIF

Mt. Blanc

Mt. Alben

◉ VERTOVA

COURMAYEUR

◉ AOSTA

BERGAMO ◉

VENICE ◉

◉ TURIN

N

GENOVA
◉

COL DE
TENDE
◉

FINALE LIGURE
◉

KEY TRIP NOTES

REGION/LOCATION(S):
Courmayeur and Mont Blanc massif,
Vertova and Bergamasque Alps, and
Cortina d'Ampezzo and the Dolomites.

CATEGORY:
3 x weekend-overnighters

DISTANCE:
220 km (137 mi)

TERRAIN:
Road/gravel

SKILL LEVEL:
Intermediate–advanced

HIGHLIGHTS:
Mountain hut (*rifugio*) nights, cable car
climbs, swimming in glacier meltwater

below Mont Blanc, Courmayeur cafes
and Alpine Museum, famous road
passes and rough-stuff gravel tracks.

ESSENTIAL GEAR/EQUIPMENT:
Gravel bike (or a bike capable of riding
off smooth tarmac), Walter Bonatti's
The Mountains of My Life, bivvy bag
and sleep kit for sleeping out among
big peaks, warm layers (the route is
often exposed at high altitude, and
descents can get cold even in summer),
and camera.

RESUPPLY INFO:
Courmayeur, Vertova, and Cortina
d'Ampezzo for shops, cafes, and bars.
Mountain huts provide dinner and
drinks. Book in advance where possible.

RIDE SEASON:
May–October

CONTRIBUTOR / RIDER INFO

A miserable night bivvy-ing out in
the Scottish Highlands had Stefan
and Jordan Gibbons first discussing
a Walter Bonatti-themed trip. They
had both read about his trademark
winter bivouac nights in his book,
The Mountains of My Life, and soon
began plotting Bonatti locations
in northern Italy across several maps.
Dan Easton, photographer and cycling
enthusiast, joined them for the week
of climber-inspired bike adventures.

EXPLORING THE VENETO PEAKS OF MONTE GRAPPA AND PASUBIO

ROUTE
GRAPPA MASSIF HUTPACKING

LOCATION
ITALY

AS TRIP BASES go, the Veneto city of Bassano del Grappa in the heart of rolling prosecco country is up there with the best: train links to the main travel centers of Venice or Verona; shop, bar, and cafe-filled piazzas; and it's home to Nardini, Italy's oldest distillery. Bortolo Nardini founded the distillery in 1779 on the Ponte Vecchio, the iconic bridge originally designed by Andrea Palladio in the sixteenth century. Nardini has been making grappa in Bassano for centuries, and their cozy locals bar on the banks of the Brenta river—an important strategic waterway for connecting the mountains with Veneto cities—makes for a fine pre-trip toast location.

The "grappa" in Grappa Massif does not just refer to the alcoholic drink whose provenance lies in these alpine foothills, but also to the range of 2,000-meter (6,562-foot) mountains, and in particular, the famous Monte Grappa (1,775 meters [5,824 feet]), whose incredible high point overlooking the Veneto plain would be the first pit stop. Given the region's storied and complicated history as a strategic location for competing Italian and Austrian forces during the First World War, any of the *rifugios* dotted around the summit are an interesting yet stunning overnight destination. Make sure to explore the network of roads and tracks, and fit in a visit to the Military Memorial Monument at the summit. You cannot miss it. →

"A WEEKEND HUT-TO-HUT BIKEPACKING TOUR DISCOVERING TWO SPECIAL HIGHPOINTS IN THE VENETIAN ALPS."

CHALLENGING RIDING UP TO MOUNTAIN SUMMIT HUTS MEANS A MORNING COFFEE, AND CAFE STOPS ARE A BIG PART OF THE BIKEPACKING DAY.

Descending the famed cycling flanks of Monte Grappa in the early morning while hundreds of riders pedal their way up is like an advertisement for this region's popular road cycling culture and heritage. Next up for the Grappa bikepackers was the Pasubio valley and Monte Pasubio, whose summit *rifugio* was the destination for the evening, 80 kilometers (50miles) west and 2,100 meters (6,890 feet) up, via the coffee stop hilltop-walled town of Marostica. When planning bikepacking trips, you might want to avoid busier tarmac roads, but sometimes they are essential for knitting together amazing sections of routes and getting between places quicker. Plus, nothing beats the feeling of a stretch of groomed tarmac after a stack of challenging off-road kilometers. A prime example of worthy road riding is the section across the Veneto plain from Marostica to the foot of Passo Xomo, which enables a day's transition between the Monte Grappa and Pasubio summits.

Dusky tones silhouetted the surrounding peaky landscape from the terrace of the *rifugio*. The ride across and up took longer than anticipated. Of course it did; rides always take longer in the mountains, especially with a large group. Whichever way you climb Pasubio by bike, you are in for a challenging treat. From Passo Xomo, take either the chunky gravel Strada degli Scarubbi from the west, or the more rideable and historic gravel Strada degli Eroi—known as the "Road of the Heroes"—from the south, a passage built in 1922 after the First World War to provide the summit area with vehicle and supply access. With their uniquely steep drops, tunnels and galleries, and gravel switchbacks, both these routes will etch into your adventure-cycling memory. And the evening and morning spent at the summit *rifugio* is just something else. It is well worth carrying a small bottle of Nardini grappa to share around after a hearty mountaintop polenta dinner as the light finally fades around the Venetian Alps theater. ○

KEY TRIP NOTES

REGION/LOCATION(S):
Venetian Alps

CATEGORY:
2–3 day escape

DISTANCE:
200 km (125 mi)

TERRAIN:
Road/gravel

SKILL LEVEL:
Intermediate–advanced

HIGHLIGHTS:
Bassano del Grappa, Monte Grappa road climbs, Monte Pasubio gravel climbs, *rifugio* overnighters, mountaintop polenta meals, and sunset grappa-tasting sessions.

ESSENTIAL GEAR/EQUIPMENT:
Sunscreen, water bottles, warm jackets and off-bike *rifugio* clothes, and hip flask.

RESUPPLY INFO:
Bassano del Grappa, Marostica, Thiene, and Schio. *Rifugios* provide evening dinner and breakfast—make sure to book in advance, if possible.

RIDE SEASON:
May–October

CONTRIBUTOR/RIDER INFO

The Grappa Massif Tour was a Pannier.cc experience in collaboration with cycle-clothing company PEdALED, who are based in Veneto and wanted to host riders in their bikepacking backyard—the Venetian Alps from Bassano del Grappa.

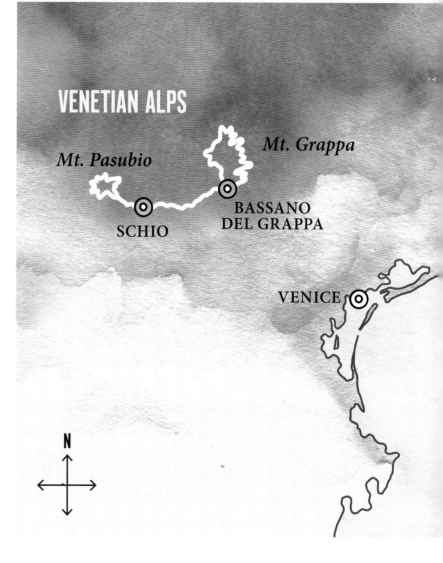

VENETIAN ALPS

Mt. Pasubio   Mt. Grappa

SCHIO   BASSANO DEL GRAPPA

VENICE

N

DISCOVERING THE ORTLER ALPS' PASSES, TRACKS, AND HUTS

ROUTE
LOOPING THE ORTLER

LOCATION
ITALY

AT 3,095 METERS (12,812 FEET) above sea level, the Ortler is the highest mountain peak in the Eastern Alps, and the namesake of the Ortler Alps. The highest, glacier-ridden areas of this range remain the domain of intrepid hikers, alpinists, and even summer skiers. But for an adventure biker, there is a whole network of famous road passes and undiscovered rough-stuff tracks, leading riders up high into these magnificent mountains. In terms of modern history, not only were Ortler's flanks the site of the highest trenches in history, separating the Italian and Austrian armies in the First World War, but also the local training ground for Reinhold Messner, the mountaineer who was

the first to climb all 14 peaks over 8,000 meters (26,000 feet). Somewhat of a local celebrity, Messner owns a small farm and restaurant-bar in the village of Sulden.

Within the Stelvio National Park, the incredible Stelvio Pass formed the spine of this journey. Given the surrounding terrain, it is the only real route option without crampons, but if a road is closed for half of the year, you can expect it to be special! While a bridle path had existed for centuries before, the Stelvio road in its current form was built by the Austrian government from 1820 to 1824 to connect the former Austrian province of Lombardy with the rest of the country. Now, merely 13 meters (43 feet) behind →

FAMOUS PRO-ROAD
CYCLING CLIMBS AND
REMOTE ROUGH-STUFF
MOUNTAIN TRACKS—
THIS REGION HAS IT ALL.
A BIKEPACKING GEM.

"CHALLENGING? YES. UNKNOWN? YES. STEEP? YES. BUT THE REWARDS ARE WELL WORTH IT."

the Col de l'Iseran in France, the Stelvio Pass—the Ortler Alps' jewel—is the second-highest paved road pass in the Alps, at 2,757 meters (9,045 feet), and connects South Tyrol to various valleys, Bormio, and routes into Switzerland. Riding the lengthy, meandering pass at a quiet time of day makes for a memorable, challenging experience.

Leave Bormio at dawn for the leg out to Sulden, Madritschjoch, and incredible views of "das Dreigestirn"—the impressive lineup of Königspitze, Zebru, and Ortler—which is German for " the three heavenly bodies." The climb is tough; the descent is incredible. If needed, a cable car runs up to the hut. Seeking and continuing on these gravel tracks where the tarmac roads end is where the real adventure lies. Challenging? Yes. Unknown? Yes. Steep? Yes. But the rewards are well worth it. Fred Wright, intrepid cyclist and author of *Rough Stuff Cycling in the Alps* sums up this pursuit perfectly: "A cyclist will often look at a map, see a road running up into the mountains and ending there … often they need not be discouraged, and that with the

right equipment and variable amount of effort they can go up the valley and over into another valley, then get back on their bike and on their way." The varying terrain on this Ortler trip is well-suited for an adventure/gravel bike, which is a cross between a road and mountain bike with capable geometries, clearance for suitable tires, and gearing to tackle tougher terrain—as at home on the Stelvio Pass as the Stelvio rough stuff.

After descending back to Sulden, ride the Stelvio back toward Bormio but drop off slightly earlier and head for the gravel around Lago di Cancano and San Giacomo at the head of the snaking Torre Fraele Pass—the exciting finish line of the 2020 Giro d'Italia Maglia Rosa stage. The final, southern leg of the loop involves a special gravel ride up to Rifugio Pizzini in the shadows of the Gran Zebru, with the Ortler peeking out along the distant ridge.

If you want to continue your exploration by bike, you could extend your trip to include the nearby Gavia and Umbrail passes. This region really is a bikepacking playground. ○

DESCENDING ROUGH-STUFF TRACKS BELOW THE ORTLER, ZEBRU, AND KÖNIGSPITZE PEAKS.

HUTPACKING TIPS

- Phone ahead to make sure the huts are open and have space. You can let them know to expect you—and your appetite.
- Reserve a bed early.
- Get on the good side of the hut warden as soon as possible.
- Use the boot/kit room. Hut slippers are a must.
- Bring: cash (more than you think—the infrastructure required to run these huts justifies it), sketchbook (for hut stamps, diary keeping, and sketching), towel, sleeping bag liner, ear plugs (communal sleeping), headlamp, wet wipes.
- Always ask to sample the hut's home-brew *génépi* or local liquor.
- B. Y. O. B.—bring your own breakfast. Dinners are hearty, tasty, and amazing. Breakfasts not so much, especially to set you up for a day in the mountains.
- Do not leave cheese in communal spaces!

WAKING UP EARLY IS ALWAYS WORTH IT ON A TRIP. NOT TO RUSH, BUT TO APPRECIATE THE SURROUNDINGS—AND COLLECT WATER FOR A DAWN BREW.

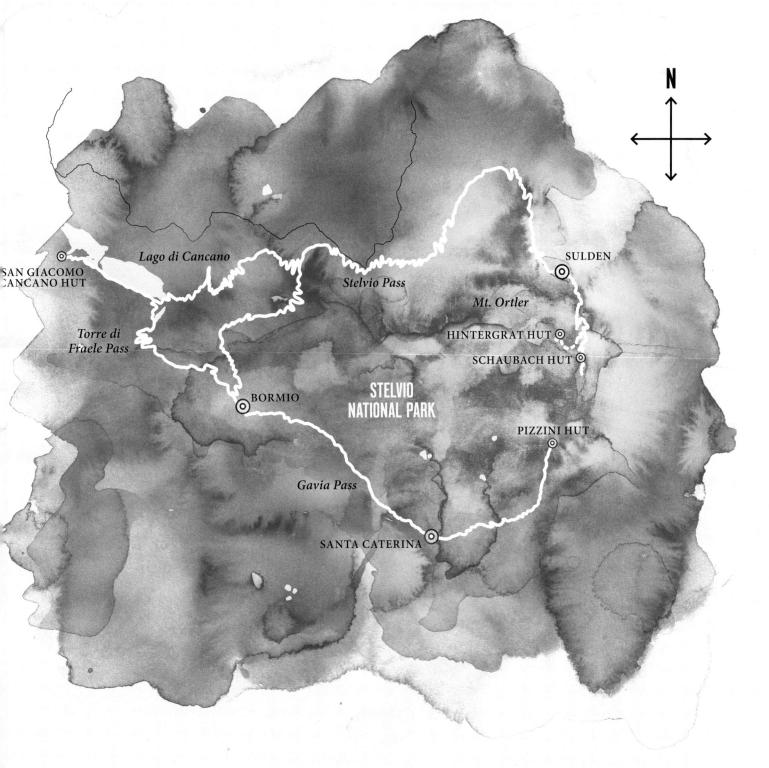

N

SAN GIACOMO
CANCANO HUT

Lago di Cancano

Stelvio Pass

SULDEN

Mt. Ortler

HINTERGRAT HUT

SCHAUBACH HUT

*Torre di
Fraele Pass*

STELVIO
NATIONAL PARK

BORMIO

PIZZINI HUT

Gavia Pass

SANTA CATERINA

KEY TRIP NOTES

REGION/LOCATION(S):
Stelvio National Park, Ortler Alps

CATEGORY:
2–3 day escape

DISTANCE:
200 km (125 mi)

TERRAIN:
Road/gravel

SKILL LEVEL:
Intermediate–advanced

HIGHLIGHTS:
Rifugio génépi nightcaps, *canederli*
(a Tyrolean bread dumpling) lunches,
Braulio distillery and tasting tours,

riding the Stelvio Pass at dawn
and dusk, and dead-end gravel
tracks into the mountains.

ESSENTIAL GEAR/EQUIPMENT:
Kompass 072 map, *Rough Stuff
Cycling in the Alps* book, journal
for hut stamps, and camera.

RESUPPLY INFO:
Bormio is the main base for this trip, and
there is not much en route. But the two
longer legs pass through Sulden and Santa
Caterina di Valfurva, which have cafes,
restaurants, shops, and cash points. There
are also a couple of bars and restaurants
dotted along the Stelvio Pass. *Rifugios*
provide evening meals and breakfasts, but

be sure to book in advance and let
them know you are definitely coming.

RIDE SEASON:
June–September

CONTRIBUTOR/RIDER INFO

The Ortler Loop was a Pannier.cc
production inspired by *Rough Stuff
Cycling in the Alps* pioneer Fred Wright.
A three-day bikepack trip was plotted
from his gravel guidebook. Joining
Stefan and David Sear were their pals,
tiramisu lovers and experienced riders
Jordan Gibbons (photographer), Beth
Hodge, and Jess Duffy.

PASS-STORMING THE ZILLERTAL ALPS

→

ROUTE
INNSBRUCK HUTPACKING

LOCATION
AUSTRIA/ ITALY

WHY DO WE climb mountains? "Because they are there" is generally the mountaineer's classic response. This bikepacking trip format is arguably the cycling equivalent of summiting a peak—riding up to the where the tarmac ends and linking up passes on foot. Call it "pass-storming" or "thru-biking." Whatever you name it, the pursuit makes for a challenging and rewarding escape.

Selecting a start point for a trip like this is always a big consideration, especially with folks traveling from various places and needing some sort of base to set up bikes and bikepacking kits. Converging and commencing from a major transport hub like Innsbruck, which is located on the edge of an alpine playground, sure makes for a straightforward start. Planning circular routes means logistics are slightly easier—you can leave bike boxes and other items from your travel kit behind to pick up on your return, for example. Sometimes it is worth working backwards on a trip: choosing an accessible start point and plotting a route around that. This trip from Innsbruck was about simply riding

in the mountains, connecting Austria and Italy through the stunning alpine arena at Pfitscherjoch/Passo di Vizze at 2,276 meters (7,467 feet). The route incorporated the two extremes of bikepacking: from valley bottom paved cycle paths to strenuous alpine singletrack hike-a-bikes. Or, as the guys coined it, "mild to wild."

The planned route was 250 kilometers (155 miles) up into the Zillertal Alps via Mayrhofen, a small town in the Zillertal Valley. The day before they embarked, Anna MacLeod, Chris Lansley, David Sear, and Stefan met for pizza in Innsbruck. All the bikes were out of their boxes, semi-built and packed, alongside the classic "night before" piles of supplies strewn across the floor and table. Setting off early the next morning, the group took a quick ride up architect Zaha Hadid's network of glacier-inspired Nordpark Railway Stations, which made for a fun descent on loaded bikes back down to the city. It was also a great detour before mild gravel, farm tracks, and designated cycle paths led the group out of the city center, where they followed

the quick flowing white water of the Inn river on their way up into the Zillertal Valley. With nearly 2,000 meters (6,561 feet) of climbing to the overnight hut, it was a challenging day—average speeds can dwindle down to 5–10 kph (3–6 mph) for off-road riding and hiking. Beyond the Alpine town and winter resort of Mayrhofen, the ride became really special—the "wild" they were after. A hot chocolate in the hut at the Schlegeisspeicher glacial reservoir marked the halfway point of the climb, and the start of the real rough-stuff ascent up to their overnight hut.

The *rifugio*—the Italian term for a type of mountain cabin or hut usually only accessible by foot—perched high above, silhouetted on the dusky horizon at the Pfitscherjoch/Passo di Vizze, on the border of Italy and Austria. Although this area of South Tyrol is an Italian province, there is a great mix of Italian and German spoken here, making it hard to know what the major preference is. Official sources say that the first language of inhabitants is 70 percent German, 25 percent Italian, and 5 percent →

WILD: CROSSING THE BORDER BETWEEN AUSTRIA AND ITALY HIGH UP AT PFITSCHERJOCH—GRAVEL RIDING PARADISE.

MILD: REJOINING THE TARMAC, AND CIVILIZATION, AT THE VALLEY BOTTOM—ONWARDS TO BRUNECK.

THE MOUNTAINS
AROUND INNSBRUCK
OFFER A GREAT
INTRO RIDE BEFORE
GOING DEEPER IN
THE ZILLERTAL ALPS.

Ladin, the region's own language. Prior to the military building more established tracks in the 1930s, it is said that the local alpine clubs established the first trails up to this point during the mid 1800s, when climbing, hiking, and leisure activities were becoming more popular. The hut is now run by the fifth generation of the Volgger family, and was originally built in 1888 by their great-grandfather, Alois Rainer.

Apart from the interwar years when it was taken over by the Italian military, the hut has largely remained open since then, offering incredible shelter in the most special of alpine arenas. Rebuilt in 2012, the Pfitscherjoch hut is a comfortable place to spend the night and a great sight for tired eyes at the end of a long day on the bikes. From a bikepacking perspective, huts like these are perfect places to stay—they have a bike room for more than 30 bikes, hot showers, great food and drink, and even a lake for post—or pre-ride swims. There is not much more you could ask for on a weekend bike adventure. Time to seek out a mountain hut (or two) to aim for on your next bikepacking escape. ○

THIS REGION IS MADE FOR
BIKEPACKING—GRAVEL
TRACKS, MOUNTAIN PASSES,
AND NEXT LEVEL URBAN CYCLE
PATHS AND INFRASTRUCTURE.

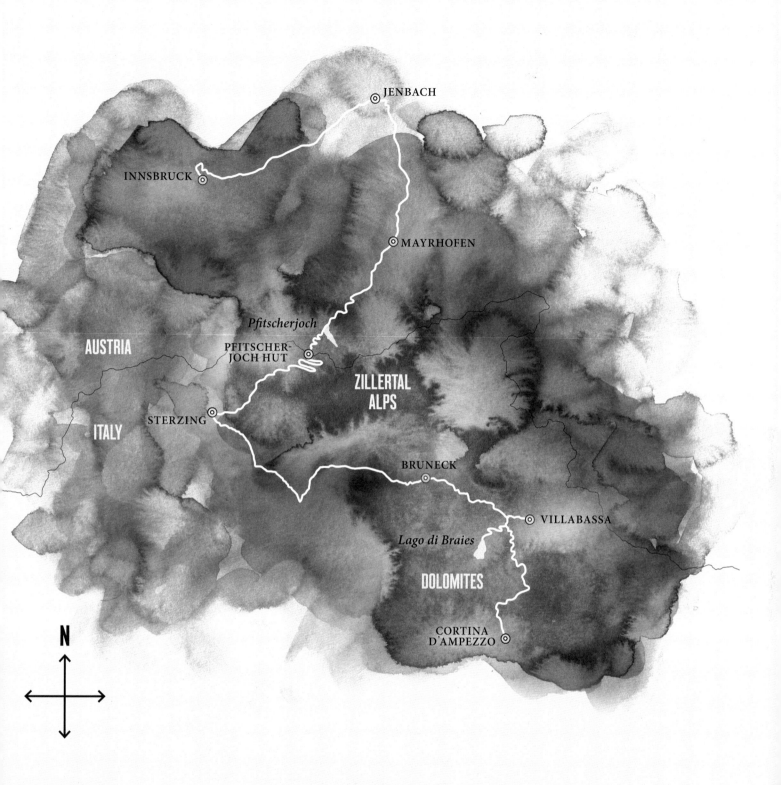

JENBACH

INNSBRUCK

MAYRHOFEN

Pfitscherjoch

AUSTRIA

PFITSCHER-
JOCH HUT

ITALY

ZILLERTAL
ALPS

STERZING

BRUNECK

VILLABASSA

Lago di Braies

DOLOMITES

CORTINA
D'AMPEZZO

N

KEY TRIP NOTES

REGION/LOCATION(S):
Zillertal Alps

CATEGORY:
Weekender-overnighter

DISTANCE:
180 km (112 mi)

TERRAIN:
Road/gravel

SKILL LEVEL:
Intermediate-advanced

HIGHLIGHTS:
Exploring Innsbruck and the Nordpark

Railway Stations, Pfitscherjoch/Passo di Vizze challenging hike-a-bike, pass sunsets, mountain hut overnights, ice-cold swims, Tyrolean *Speck,* and Zillertal cheese picnics

ESSENTIAL GEAR/EQUIPMENT:
Warm hut clothes, swim kit, hiking shoes, and snacks for the climb.

RESUPPLY INFO:
Innsbruck, Mayrhofen, San Giacomo, and Brennero. The mountain huts offer meals, but be sure to book in advance and keep in contact with the hut wardens/hosts.

RIDE SEASON:
May–October

CONTRIBUTOR/RIDER INFO

Innsbruck Hutpacking was a Pannier.cc production, tying in with a trip to ride the Dolomiti Superbike, Italy's most popular mountain bike event, on gravel bikes. Anna MacLeod and Chris Lansley joined David Sear and Stefan on the trip, bringing their own off-road and coffee-making skills.

TRAIL HUNTING FROM MOUNTAINS TO SEA

→

ROUTE
ALLGÄU TO FINALE LIGURE

LOCATION
GERMANY, AUSTRIA, SWITZERLAND, AND ITALY

THE MOUNTAIN AIR was impossibly calm. All that broke the silence was the sound of Alex Fuchs and Mathis Burger's tires on tarmac, which sounded like velcro being ripped open. The effect of the wide, sticky mountain bike rubber on the tarmac was similar to velcro too. Every pedal stroke felt like starting from scratch, momentum lost as quickly as it was generated. Even with the rear shock locked out, climbing was not exactly their full suspension enduro bikes' forte. Alex looked back and cursed. To make matters worse, they were each hauling a 28 kilogram (62 pound) trailer up the 2,066-meter-high (6,778-foot) high San Bernardino Pass in Switzerland, and were just a couple of days into an epic crossing of the Alps. Starting at their home in Allgäu, Germany, they planned to finish at the Mediterranean Sea and the mountain-biking mecca of Finale Ligure, linking together some of the best trails in the world as they made their way southwest through the mountains.

Bike touring is all about compromise. As an example, the more we take, the more comfortable our time is off the bike. But every creature comfort adds to the weight we have to carry. It is no coincidence that most bikepacking and touring is done on rigid bikes. In general, they are lighter and more efficient, and there is less to go wrong in the wilderness. Although these bikes can transport us to the greatest mountain-biking destinations in the world, the downside is they are less than ideal when it comes to maximizing fun when we are there.

Fueled by visions of pristine alpine singletrack, slicing past ice blue glacial lakes and through wildflower meadows, Alex and Mathis decided to flip convention. Their full suspension enduro mountain bikes were optimize for speed and fun on technical off-road descents. They fitted trailers—loaded with tents and everything else needed for the best part of a month on the road—to the perfect bikes for enjoying the trails and accepted that they would have to just deal with the extra weight.

Nice idea in theory, but they had 1,400 kilometers (870 miles) and 24,000 meters (78,740 feet) of height gain to tick off in just 22 days. Their legs already felt battered when they pulled into Lago Maggiore later. →

BIKE TOURING, ENDURO STYLE: UNHITCH THE TRAILER, MAKE CAMP, TAKE FLIGHT!

"BIKE TOURING
IS ALL ABOUT
COMPROMISE."

The lake spans the border between Switzerland and Italy, and the hills above the lake contain a spiderweb of interconnected trails—perfect mountain biking. The next day, ignoring complaining quads, the pair unhitched their trailers and set off to explore. It felt as though someone had snuck a motor onto their bikes overnight. Each pedal stroke threw them forward as they climbed unencumbered through thick forests to hilltop villages. With nowhere else to climb, they finally could point their front wheels down a trail, plumes of dust following them on a frenzied plummet back to the shores of the lake.

This pattern of a few days slogging onward followed by a window of reward was repeated along their route. Lake Orta was next and then Pogno, where they discovered the most wonderful flow trails and human kindness to match as strangers invited them to dinner. After a couple more days they would move on, always balancing the desire to appreciate each location with an eagerness to reach the next trail destination.

The days in-between somehow became easier. Physically they remained hard, but the pair mentally readjusted to the task at hand, and at some point it felt as though their legs resigned themselves to their fate and stopped voicing their discontent once they had warmed up each day. Fueled by €1 roadside espressos, the duo would ride along valleys before climbing the next mountain pass,

FROM THE MOUNTAINS
TO THE MED: THE PAIR
WERE THERE FOR THE
TRAILS, BUT SOME OF
THE ROADS WERE PRETTY
SPECTACULAR TOO.

haring down the other side, their eyes always drawn upward, scanning the flanks of hills for telltale ribbons of singletrack.

They spent an entire week exploring the magnificent Aosta Valley. With their trailers once again left behind, they climbed to 2,500 meters (8,202 feet) and traversed along balcony trails that gave huge panoramic views across to the Mont Blanc massif range, almost close enough to touch. Over and over, they were rewarded with primo high

alpine flow all the way down to gelatos and beers back in the valley.

Time was against the pair, though, and they still had a tough traverse of the Southern Alps to reach Finale Ligure. The town sits where the mountains meet the sea, and beyond its walls is a network of trails that weaves nearly all the way down to the beach. Alex and Mathis spent a final few days riding laps there, content that their journey was complete, but the fun could be eked out a little longer. ○

153

NOT YOUR AVERAGE BIKEPACKING BIKES. RECOVERING IN THE SHADE AFTER ANOTHER PASS CROSSING.

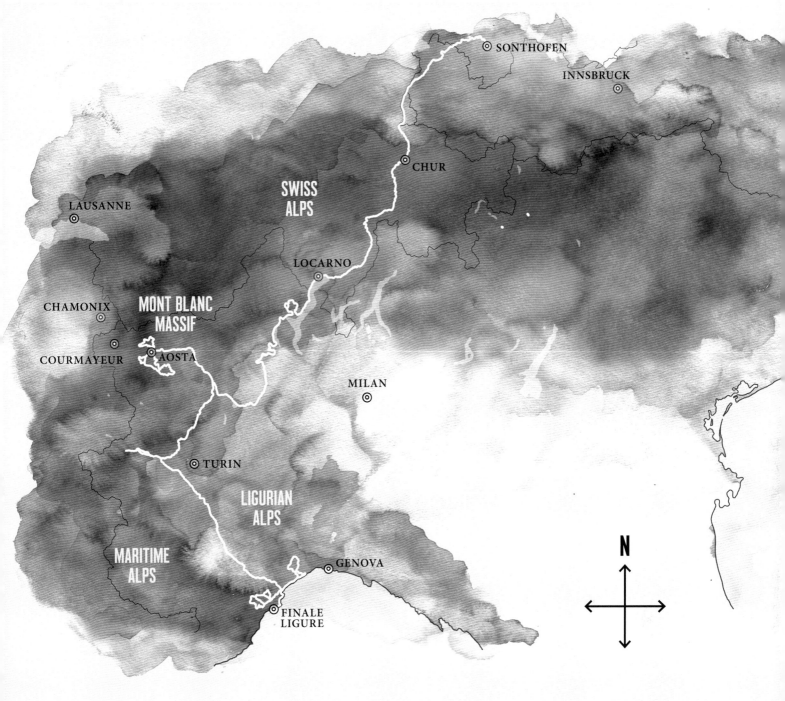

KEY TRIP NOTES

REGION/LOCATION(S):
A crossing of the Alps via Germany, Austria, Switzerland, and Italy, taking in the best mountain bike trails en route, including those in Lago Maggiore, Aosta Valley, and Finale Ligure.

CATEGORY:
"Tour and shred" point-to-point trip

DISTANCE:
1,400 km (870 mi)

TERRAIN:
Roads connecting mountain bike trails, and everything from woodland flow trails to high alpine technical and rocky singletrack.

SKILL LEVEL:
Advanced. The route covers 24,000 vertical meters (78,740 feet) of climbing on a bike that is not designed to be an efficient mile-muncher.

HIGHLIGHTS:
The best of both worlds: crossing a mountain range by bike, but getting to enjoy its trails to the maximum.

ESSENTIAL GEAR/EQUIPMENT:
To make the most of the alpine trails, a full suspension enduro mountain bike is recommended, with 140 millimeters or more of travel. Resilient tires may feel draggy on the road but will be welcomed on the rockiest descents. A trailer makes for the easiest switching between touring and shredding mode: it's simple to unhitch and stow at a campsite. The route, or a variation of it, could be completed using hotels and guest houses, but camp gear allows more flexibility. Bring a waterproof jacket and a warmer layer for the evenings.

RESUPPLY INFO:
The route passes through towns and villages along its entirety. Village shops are often closed on Sundays in the Alps.

RIDE SEASON:
July–September

CONTRIBUTOR/RIDER INFO

Alex Fuchs is a self-taught professional photographer from the Allgäu region of Germany. Growing up in the mountains meant that he has always felt a strong connection to them and is happiest when riding or shooting up high. He took this trip with Mathis Burger.

UNEARTHING A MODERNIST HISTORY IN THE ALPES-MARITIMES

→

ROUTE
BUNKER BIKEPACKING

LOCATION
FRANCE AND ITALY

A HEARTY PRE-RIDE breakfast is essential for bikepacking in the stunning but challenging terrain of the Alpes-Maritimes, and a bucket of *chouquettes* alongside a tray of espressos in the dawning Côte d'Azur sun makes a great start. With bunker bivvy kits, *vin*, *pain*, and Boursin strapped to their bikes, the five-strong squad set off from the beachfront straight up into the mountains that rise sharply around the decadent port city. Ahead was a three-day round trip ride to Col de Tende, a long-fortified, strategic high point now on the border between Italy and France. The plan was to bivvy out for one night and stay at a mountain refuge on the other to experience the best of both worlds.

The bunker fortifications in the Alpes-Maritimes formed the southern extension known as the Little Maginot Line, built out of paranoia that Italy would invade France over the Alps and take Nice, France's jewel on the south coast. Of course, the Italians under Mussolini responded by building their own wall, the Vallo Alpino (Alpine Wall), to protect their 1,850-kilometer-long (1,150-mile) borders with France, Switzerland, Austria, and Yugoslavia. As a result, there was a bunker-off between Italy and France at each of the weak points along this mountainous border. Once you know to look for them, bunkers appear everywhere, from small cloches in Menton and along the Col de la Madone climb to *gros ouvrage* complexes camouflaged among the hills above Sainte-Agnès and Castillon, which were built in the early 1930s at costs upwards of millions of francs. However, bunker building, and military infrastructure in general, offers a surprising benefit for adventure cyclists: a whole network of special roads and gravel tracks that run wild in the mountains, and that would not otherwise exist.

Knowing the weather will be warm and dry for a few days makes it a lot easier to prepare for a bikepacking trip. The typical kit for bivvying includes a bivvy bag, sleeping →

BUNKER HUNTING AT BAISSE DE PEYREFIQUE—THE HIGH POINT OF THE TRIP—ON THE RIDGE LINE TO COL DE TENDE.

bag, sleeping mat, warm jacket, and hat. The group's Monte Grosso bivvy setups varied. Some opted to just bring warm down jackets and leave their sleeping bags in Nice, while some left behind bivvy bags and slept out in sleeping bags. Others forgot their sleeping mats. Guess who did not have a good night's sleep? Bikepacking Rule No. 1: never leave your sleeping mat at home. They are the number one piece of

camp kit for warmth and comfort.

The morning's ride from Vallauris to the Baisse de Peyre-fique—the highest point of the trip at 2,000 meters (6,562 feet)—was a real standout stretch of riding. The steep singletrack roads round and cross the head of the river valley as the surface changes to gravel. On these high alpine pastures, cattle bells ring and echo around to signal the entrance to this

bunker-filled pass. Along the ridge, toward Col de Tende, the crowds slowly build to a climax at the Chalet Marmotte (1,800 meters [5,900 feet]), which heaves with Italian tourists either sunbathing post-lunch or honking at each other in the crowded car park. Plates of polenta were demolished at a restaurant, below which 48 hairpin bends of the Col de Tende gravel road run for seven kilometers (four miles),

signaling a joyful exit from the high mountains.

The irony of a bunker is that it cannot easily be erased, but its subterranean design and remote locale mean it cannot be reappropriated as a useful building either. As author Max Leonard writes in his book *Bunker Research*, these decommissioned spaces "are still watchful, entirely visible and yet invisible, neutralized and domesticated, left to slowly decay and be overrun by the landscape."

It is interesting to think about how, a few hundred years from now, intrepid cyclists will continue to seek out these bunker sites. They might imagine the rationale—or lack of—behind them, try to understand how they worked and what life was like here centuries ago.

Do you have a niche bikepacking tour theme to beat bunkers? ○

NO MATTER THE HEAT OR CLIMBING, THERE IS NOT MUCH A CYCLIST'S PORTION OF MOUNTAIN HUT POLENTA AND A COLD DRINK WON'T FIX.

BUNKER GUIDE, MAX, DESCENDING TO THE VALLEY FLOOR ON THE VAST NETWORK OF "ROUTES-STRATEGIQUES" MILITARY ROADS.

"ONCE YOU KNOW TO LOOK FOR THEM, BUNKERS APPEAR EVERYWHERE."

COL DE TENDE

MARITIME
ALPS

CASTERINO

TENDE

LA BRIGUE

MERCANTOUR
NATIONAL PARK

BREIL-SUR-ROYA

SOSPEL

MENTON

MONACO

NICE

FRENCH RIVIERA

N

KEY TRIP NOTES

REGION/LOCATION(S):
Alpes-Maritimes, Nice

CATEGORY:
2–3 day escape

DISTANCE:
200 km (125 mi)

TERRAIN:
Road/gravel

SKILL LEVEL:
Intermediate–advanced

HIGHLIGHTS:
Exploring Nice, riding switchback passes straight up into the mountains from the beach, bunker hunting, bunker bivvys, learning about the modern history of the region, mountain hut polenta, Col de Tende, gravel military access roads, boulangerie lunches, and Roya river swims.

ESSENTIAL GEAR/EQUIPMENT:
Bunker Research book, sunscreen, water carriers, bivvy kit, bread, wine, and Boursin. Mercantour National Park is a no-flame area, so please follow this rule and do not use camp stoves.

RESUPPLY INFO:
Before setting off, stock up in Nice. Otherwise there is Sospel, Casterino, and a couple of villages dotted through the Roya Valley. Mountain refuges will provide dinner. Booking ahead is advisable.

RIDE SEASON:
May–October

CONTRIBUTOR/RIDER INFO

The Bunker Bikepack was a collaborative trip between Max Leonard (author and bunker guide), Remi Clermont and Ali McKee (Nice locals and Alpes-Maritimes road/gravel connoisseurs), Antton Miettinen (photographer), and Stefan (bunker bivvy host).

HOW TO TRAVEL IN A GROUP

*Stefan Amato has been organizing and leading bikepacking
trips for the last decade, namely for the outfit he founded in 2012, Pannier.cc.
Stefan runs through the ins and outs of bikepacking as a group.*

Bringing the outdoors and people together is what cycling is all about. "Time in a group, however big or small, is a reminder that riding bikes is fun. Add a multiday bikepacking route and you've got a recipe for adventure, challenge, and memorable times," says Stefan. Sharing is a big bonus of having companions: sharing motivation, confidence, experience, and what and how others ride, pack, cook, eat, camp, or even wheelie. "If joining an organized bikepacking tour or event is not your camp mug of tea, try joining a local cycling club or national organization like Rough-Stuff Fellowship, or finding other like-minded bikepackers online," says Stefan. Already got a group of pals that are keen for a local overnighter or an escape in the mountains? Great. Here are some things to consider.

The right vibe is fundamental. Make sure everyone is on the same page regarding distance, terrain, challenge, accommodations, roughing-it level, budget, and bike setup.

The size of a group affects social and riding dynamics, transport and accommodation options, "faff" time, and trail impact. Riding as a group is naturally more leisurely with a social focus, with a kind of "pack your swim kit and catapult" mindset. While it also offers collective skills, knowledge, decision-making, and safety in numbers, every extra person increases the chance of accidents and mechanical issues. If riding as a bigger group of six or more, things like avoiding big, busy main roads or built-up areas, splitting up into two easily passable groups, and being considerate and welcoming to other trail users are a must. Make sure start and end points are accessible for everyone. A circular route definitely simplifies logistics for groups.

On the road, "you'll likely end up pedaling within a snack's throw of each other, but it is natural to ride and pause at your own pace, especially off-road," says Stefan. "Sure, stick to the 'ride as fast as your slowest rider' ethos, but a good rule is to never lose sight of the person behind you." Make sure everyone is briefed on the route, and that they have it on a phone, GPS device, or scribbled in a sketchbook, alongside some checkpoints for each day. "Regrouping tends to work out naturally anyway at pinch points: high points, low points, swim plunge pools, and resupply points. We've definitely had it where the faster road cyclists have had their eyes opened to the slow, social bikepacking way," says Stefan.

While it is best for everyone to be as self-sufficient as possible when it comes to packing, knocking helmets together to streamline kit and share the load is well worth doing to avoid having 12 pumps and no carbs. Make a communal list of tools and spares, cooking kit, shelter, and food and drink supplies, and leave space on your bike. Assigning roles, like camp chef, barista, or route master can help reduce dawdling in a group. If cooking as a group, check dietary requirements and allergies. "Vegetarian meals are the way to go for bikepacking, simply from a hygiene perspective," says Stefan. "Make sure to do a great job, but don't do too great of a job, or else you'll be making coffee for everyone, every day, every trip!" ○

→

GOOD TO KNOW

TYPICAL GROUP RIDING DAY:
50–120 km at 10–12 kph
(30–75 mi at 6–8 mph) over
decent terrain

GOLDEN RULES—GROUP:
• Fixed dates. Clear the calendar for pals, or book onto an organized tour/event
• Share mindsets, the same bike. setups, the load, and routes. Factor in varied paces by outlining checkpoints and regrouping rules.
• Test and challenge. Integrate big climbs, unknown tracks and trails, or bigger distances. Venturing out of comfort zones always bonds a group, and makes memories.

THREE THINGS TO TAKE—GROUP:
• The best snacks, drinks, and bikepacking hacks. It's a competition— you know that, right? B. Y. O. M.—bring your own mug—and spork for shared meals and snack stops.
• A smartphone for contact, navigation, and documenting the trip
• Specific spares for your bike
• Earplugs

"UNE GRANDE TRAVERSÉE DU JURA"

ROUTE
CROSSING THE JURA

LOCATION
FRANCE

UNSURPRISINGLY, the ski jump in Chaux-Neuve was not open in midsummer. But it was too good of a photo opportunity to pass up, so the Paris Chill Racing (PCR) Gravier crew pushed up the landing slope as far as they could, the words "CHAUX NEUVE" emblazoned across the slope above them. PCR Gravier is a collective of nine cyclists who have a penchant for adventure and unpaved routes. Their four days traversing the Jura included multiple stops, camp fires, punctures, a catapult, and a vintage Russian 16-millimeter film camera. The Krasnogorsk-3 can be manually wound up like a clock and feels like a tank both in weight and build. Filmmaker Renaud Skyronka also carried three boxes of film, stretching 90 meters (295 feet) in total, or 12 minutes of footage. They would make every frame of film count, not in terms of distance covered, but in the shared experience had along the way.

Chaux-Neuve is nestled in the middle of the Jura mountains, and the Jura themselves are in-between in many ways too. They are the middle mountains, sandwiched between the Alps and Vosges. Their peaks represent the middle ground between the rest of France and the border to Switzerland. And their height, while by no means small, is dwarfed by the Hautes-Alpes to the south. The medium mountains lure you into dangerous thinking. They must be easier, right? →

MEMORIES ARE SO
OFTEN MADE FROM THE
"MOMENTS IN BETWEEN":
TIME OFF THE BIKE,
FIXING PUNCTURES, A
FEW MINUTES OF SILENCE
BEFORE THE REST OF THE
CREW WAKE UP.

"THE ACT OF DOCUMENTING OUR TRAVELS FORCES US TO SLOW DOWN AND TAKE NOTICE OF OUR SURROUNDINGS."

Yet straining up an impossibly steep section of tarmac, the group cursed the road builders of the Jura. Did they have some kind of inferiority complex? If they cannot build the roads as high, did they think they may as well just make them steeper? Fortunately, the climbs were never too long.

The group's course roughly followed the official Grande Traversée du Jura mountain bike route, tweaked when the going got a little too rugged for their gravel bikes. They would trend southward, covering the 350 kilometers (218 miles) or so of their route over four days, which would give them time to stop for a beer or pull out the Krasnogorsk-3.

The second day of the trip unfolded through wildflower meadows and fields of cows. The group followed paths through the mountains, each view more grandiose →

169

than the last. Their target was the village of Mouthe, \and a night under a roof to break up sleeping beneath the stars. Team member Pierre Reinur's great-grandmother had bought a family home in Mouthe—known as the coldest village in France—over half a century ago. The sprawling home breathed family spirit and ached for a large party. And so PCR ended up on the terrace of the grandest house in Mouthe, getting drunk on a combination of beers and altitude before hitting the local bar for more rehydration and "the worst burger in the history of gastronomy."

The morning after their night out, the pace slowed. They cycled through more luscious valleys below stunning peaks, visited that ski jump, and hunted for the perfect spot for a final bivouac before the ride to the Bellegarde station the following day. The film whirred through the Krasnogorsk-3 at a faster pace than legs turned, but the kilometers still passed. Despite the pace, there was time to build a small campfire and cook local Morteau sausage, and simply enjoy being in the wilds before re-entry to the city.

Was it worth lugging along the Russian camera? For Renaud and the PCR crew, these journeys can be summed up in a sentence borrowed from the artist Robert Filliou: "Art is what makes life more interesting than art." For them—and maybe all of us—the act of documenting our travels, whether it is on a phone, in a notebook, or via an old camera, forces us to slow down and take notice of our surroundings. The Krasnogorsk-3 became another member of the team for a few days, one that told its stories during the weeks after as Renaud developed the meter upon meter of film captured. The result was not high-definition 4K, but the ride was not either. It was fuzzy around the edges at times, quirky, and fun. Somehow it was perfectly fitting. ○

AS THE GROUP TRENDED
SOUTHWARDS THROUGH
THE MOUNTAINS, EACH
VIEW WAS MORE GRANDIOSE
THAN THE LAST.

THE GROUP MAY NOT HAVE PACKED LIGHT, BUT THE EXTRA WEIGHT OF THE OLD RUSSIAN CAMERA WAS WORTH IT.

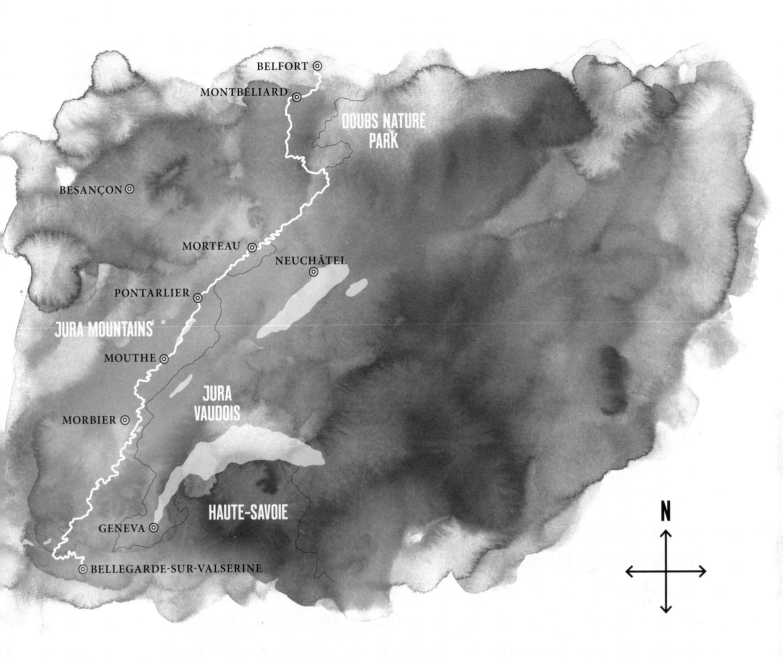

BELFORT ◉

MONTBÉLIARD ◉

DOUBS NATURE PARK

BESANÇON ◉

MORTEAU ◉

NEUCHÂTEL ◉

PONTARLIER ◉

JURA MOUNTAINS

MOUTHE ◉

JURA VAUDOIS

MORBIER ◉

HAUTE-SAVOIE

GENEVA ◉

◉ BELLEGARDE-SUR-VALSERINE

N

KEY TRIP NOTES

REGION/LOCATION(S):
North to south traverse of the Jura mountain range. The Jura lies just north and east of the Alps, running down the French-Swiss border. The route starts in Belfort and finishes in Bellegarde-sur-Valserine. Both have railway stations served by the French high-speed rail service, the TGV.

CATEGORY:
Multiday, point-to-point

DISTANCE:
327 km (203 mi)

TERRAIN:
Gravel tracks, singletrack, and quiet mountain roads

SKILL LEVEL:
Intermediate. The only difficulties encountered are very steep, but very short, slopes in some villages, as well as some areas of mountain bike track, which can be challenging on gravel bikes. However, the road is never too far away and it is always possible to find a tarmac alternative. For further inspiration, the Jura region's association has published three different routes of the official Grande Traversée du Jura track—a mountain bike version, a road version, and a touring version—all of which can be mixed and matched.

HIGHLIGHTS:
Quiet countryside in an undiscovered area of France, and a route that is easy to extend or re-calibrate on the go.

ESSENTIAL GEAR/EQUIPMENT:
Camp kit, clothing suitable for mixed mountain conditions, an old film camera, and a few friends to experience the trip with.

RESUPPLY INFO:
The route passes through multiple towns and villages with ample opportunities to resupply with local delicacies.

RIDE SEASON:
Late Spring–Autumn

CONTRIBUTOR/RIDER INFO

Paris Chill Racing Gravier is a collective of nine French cyclists, including Pierre Reinur, Simon Taulelle, Julien Sommier, and filmmaker Renaud Skyronka. The group gets together as often as possible for bikepacking trips, and as a rule, the less tarmac the happier they are. The group also has a passion for analog photography and videography.

JOURNEYING ALONG SLOVENIA'S SOČA RIVER, AND BEYOND

ROUTE
SOČA SPRINGLANDS

LOCATION
SLOVENIA

OPTIMISM IS fickle at the beginning of a bike-packing adventure into the unknown. As Duncan Philpott, David Sear, and Stefan sped east across the Veneto plain, they took nervous glances out of the train window at the snow-capped Venetian Prealp peaks, which stood shivering. Conditions were not looking great for the first stage of the trip—a ride up and over the 1,611-meter (5,285-foot) Vršič Pass (Slovenia's highest)—let alone for the next three days. Vršič is one of only two routes across to the lands of Soča, so it was an integral section of road. But after a quick call to Tanja—the guardian at Koča na Gozdu, the planned evening's mountain hut located halfway up

the pass—the optimism was back in the train carriage. "The road is clear up to three-quarters of the trip, but I can't speak for higher up," she said. No one had expected the snowstorm, and even the locals had been out plowing the pass all day. "The kitchen is open until 9 p.m., so do your best to get here before then," Tanja said. After a slow and slushy ride crossing the Slovenian border at Kranjska Gora, the squad was ready for a hearty *Jota* and *Njoki* meal, before double-checking maps, triple-guessing the weather, and recouping after the day's traveling.

In hindsight, it is more than reasonable to refer to a bikepacking trip as planned spontaneity: have no plans, except for a rough →

"ONE SHOULD NOT SEEK FOR A MERE SCRAMBLING-GROUND AMONG THE MOUNTAINS, BUT RATHER FOR THEIR SPIRIT."

— JULIUS KUGY —

LOCAL ROUTE
KNOWLEDGE IS KEY.
NEŽA TOOK US TO A
PICTURESQUE SPOT FOR
SNOW-MELT COFFEES
HIGH ON MOUNT STOL.

plan. There is a great term for this in Spanish—*vacilando*—which roughly means the act of wandering, or when the experience of travel is more important than reaching a specific destination. The idea was to spend a few days checking out various sections of the Soča spring lands for a Pannier.cc trip, with full bivvy kits and credit cards for flexibility. The aim was to piece together the famous road passes of northwestern Slovenia, with sections of the Trans Slovenia and Alpe-Adria trails to comprise a 200 kilometers (125 miles) all-road bikepacking route using the Soča river as the spine.

Julian Kugy—a Slovenian mountaineer, writer, botanist, humanist, lawyer, and officer—was renowned for his travelogues that opened up this region of the Julian Alps. His 1934 book *Alpine Pilgrimage* is a classic. Kugy explored these mountains and foothills down to the smallest larch needle (Slovenia is 60 percent forest), and he discovered and marked more than 50 new routes both solo and with local guides. And despite the book's Italian, Austrian, German, Slovenian, and Balkan place names, it is still possible to piece the peaks, passes,

and places together and follow his rough tracks.

The snow continued to fall the next morning, slowly but surely settling on the pass's tarmac outside the cozy hut. Triglav's stunning surrounding limestone peaks disappeared into the snowy skies, drifts, and forests. It seemed there would be no break in the weather to make a dash for the pass. Were the conditions any better on the other side of the pass? After waiting to see if conditions improved, the trio repacked their bikes against Laško beer crates and left the warmth of the hut. They pedaled up the last of the north side's 24 cobbled switchbacks—or serpentines, as Tanja (and every other local) called them—edging ever closer to the Soča.

Rolling virgin tracks into fresh snow, on such a humbling stretch of road, made for a great morning on the bikes. The group followed the original tracks of farmers who needed to get to pasture on the Trenta side of the valley, and folk from the rural Trenta valley who needed to stock up on supplies from Kranjska Gora. According to the information boards, the original path was

widened in 1909 for the timber industry, before being fully developed into a road by the military when the Soča (Isonzo) Front opened up. Completed in 1917, the Vršič Pass was built by 10,000 Russian prisoners of war, including the cobbled switchbacks that were likely designed for better friction during steeper sections.

It was at the highest Vršič Pass hut—the last sanctuary—where the rideable snow ended, turning to foot-deep snow and a good ol' hike-a-bike up past the final switchback sign to the 1,611-meter (5,285-foot) pass. The snow saga, followed by wet rain showers and warm sunny spells later in the day, meant experiencing "four seasons of weather in one day," according to photographer Duncan, who was trying to document the lush spring green, rugged limestone, and snow-dusted valley without getting pneumonia. Riding off the other side of the pass on clear but sodden tarmac was a big moment. Now in the spring lands of the Soča, the valley roads and gravel tracks would make the finest riding playground for the next two days, to Bovec and beyond. ○

DESCENDING THE MOUNT STOL SWITCHBACKS: UNEXPECTED SNOW ALMOST PUT A STOP TO THIS TRIP. BE PREPARED FOR YOUR PLANS TO CHANGE!

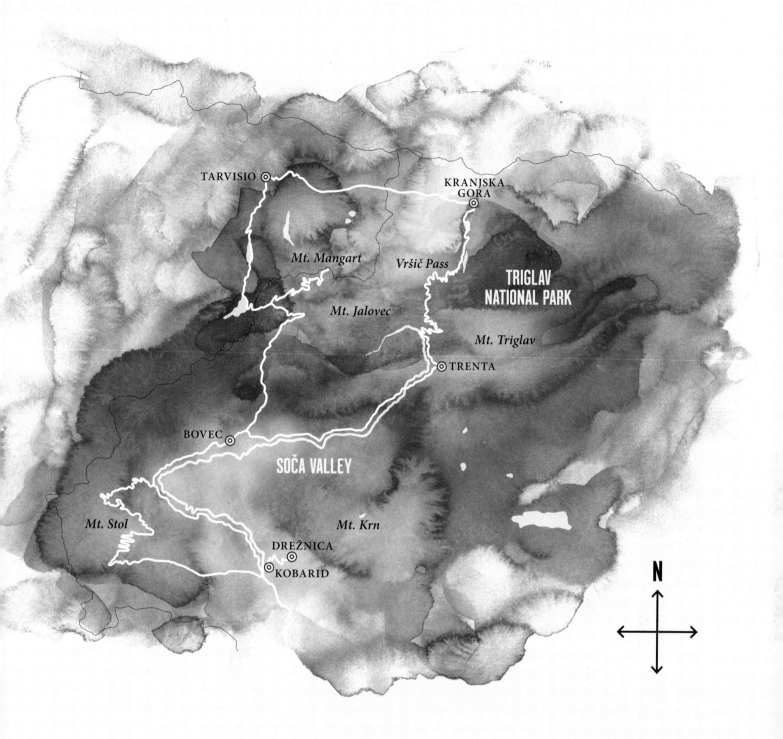

N

KEY TRIP NOTES

REGION/LOCATION(S):
Julian Alps: Triglav National Park and
Soča Valley

CATEGORY:
2–3 day escape

DISTANCE:
200 km (125 mi)

TERRAIN:
Road/gravel

SKILL LEVEL:
Intermediate

HIGHLIGHTS:
Vršič Pass, Soča swimming, Bovec,
Mount Stol lookout towers, forests,
gravel passes, pass coffees, and
Mangart Pass.

ESSENTIAL GEAR/EQUIPMENT:
Soča swim kit and pass coffee kit

RESUPPLY INFO:
Kranjska Gora, Bovec, mountain
huts (*kocas/doms*), and Kobarid. There
is not much in-between, especially out
of season.

RIDE SEASON:
May–October

CONTRIBUTOR/RIDER INFO

Soča Springlands was a Pannier.cc
production—a reconnaissance trip
to explore the lands around the Soča
Valley by bike for future bikepacking
trip routes and ideas. Joining Stefan
were Duncan Philpott (photographer)
and colleague David Sear. Snow was not
expected, and welcomed only once they
knew crossing Vršič Pass was possible—
and the group thawed out in a Bovec
pizzeria. The group also met up with
Slovenian bikepacker Neža Peterca
in Bovec for a day's riding and Mount
Stol picnic/snowmelt coffee stop.

CROSSING BORDERS: BIKEPACKING THE BALKANS

ROUTE
VIA DINARICA

LOCATION
SLOVENIA, CROATIA, BOSNIA AND HERZEGOVINA, AND MONTENEGRO

NEŽA PETERCA WAS born in Slovenia just a few years before it declared its independence from the Socialist Federal Republic of Yugoslavia in 1991. Many other former Yugoslavian states followed suit and endured fierce wars, thousands of deaths, genocide, and multiple atrocities in their bids for independence.

Growing up, Neža's parents rarely talked about the war and Slovenian schools did not seem to want to focus on such recent history. She wanted to discover more about the history of the countries that were once "home." What were the experiences of the people who lived there? How did the wars affect residents? During the scorched summer of 2019, she set off on a ride to find out.

After a long day climbing from the Croatian border, Neža and Katherine Pierce finally descended into the Blidinje Nature Park in Bosnia. They were aiming for a lakeside mountain hut and hoped they could camp there for the night. Arriving at dusk, it transpired that the hut was full with a hiking club from nearby Tuzla. "No problem," they said, and invited Neža and Katherine to join them for the evening. The group spanned generations—from teenagers to retirees—and shared bottles of *šnaps* and leftover food as they all talked late into the night. Despite the long, flowing conversations, it never felt →

THE VIA DINARICA CROSSED BORDERS SEAMLESSLY, LINKING REMOTE, HIGH VILLAGES.

like the right moment to ask about something as serious as the war though. The club invited Neža to join them for a hike to Hajdučka Vrata—"Outlaw's Gate"—the next day. The pair shrugged—why not? They were not on a schedule and maybe it would be an opportunity to find out more about the conflicts.

There is something about hiking or riding together that allows conversations to broach subjects that feel off limits at other times. Maybe it is because you tend not to be facing the other person. It feels somehow less intimate and less pressured, with longer to ponder thoughts before vocalizing them. On the long hike down from the almost perfectly circular natural rock arch that makes up Hajdučka Vrata, Neža finally felt able to broach the subject of war, particularly with the older generations of the club. Their memories were unique and personal, of course, but the sentiment was always the same. They did not describe exact battles or moments of terror, but rather the pain they still carry decades later. They were hurt to the point that all that remained was sorrow. Some were left with nothing. It is a pain most of us will never experience. There was no anger or hatred among them, rather a frustration that their country still feels fractured and fragmented, largely along ethnic and religious lines, and seems unable to unite and act as one to move forward.

Sitting in her tent later, Neža broke down in tears. It had been a defining day in her trip, and in her life. Bosnia's soil may be stained with blood, but the many innocent people who died live on in those memories shared on a dusty mountainside. Hate had ripped this beautiful country wide open, but love and understanding can—and will—rebuild it, she felt sure, knotting her hands into fists, grabbing hold of this feeling, afraid to let it go and let despair creep in.

She continued on her journey the next day. Over the coming weeks, roughly following the Via Dinarica hiking trail—interspersed with dirt road diversions when the trail became unrideable—they would hear similar stories as they linked together towns and villages through the Dinaric Alps. Their bikes disarmed locals and sparked conversations wherever they went. Conversations naturally flowed. Tales of anguish and hope. Anger and forgiveness.

Yugoslavia was a deeply flawed state, but as Neža passed seamlessly across borders on her trip, she observed that the mountains looked the same on either side of an artificial line. The trail was no different. The Croatian sheep were just as noisy as Montenegrin sheep, especially in the early hours of the morning. The people, at heart, were the same. Despite the fractures of war, she finished the trip convinced that the future has to be brighter. Differences in ethnicity, religion, and culture could be overcome. ○

MOUNTAIN LIFE WAS CAREFREE, BUT NEŽA WANTED TO EXPLORE THE TURBULENT HISTORY OF THE COUNTRIES SHE PASSED THROUGH.

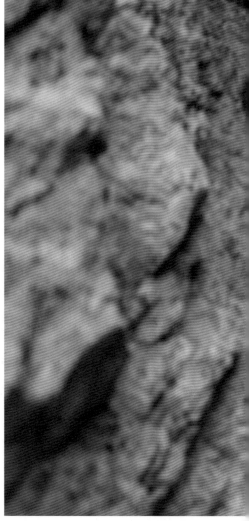

KEY TRIP NOTES

REGION/LOCATION(S):
Journey from Slovenia,
crossing the mountains
of Croatia, Bosnia,
and Montenegro

CATEGORY:
Mountain bike point-to-
point tour

DISTANCE:
1,700 km (1,056 mi)

TERRAIN:
Mostly dirt and gravel
roads, linked together
with tarmac and occasional
rougher sections.

SKILL LEVEL:
Intermediate. A long
route with some sustained
climbing, but plenty of
opportunities to ride shorter
sections as a weekend trip.

HIGHLIGHTS:
The Via Dinarica trail
is not rideable along its
entire length, but provides
incredible, scenic singletrack riding through the
mountains of the Dinaric
Alps. There are service road
options around the most
technical sections.

**ESSENTIAL
GEAR/EQUIPMENT:**
Camp kit and stove

RESUPPLY INFO:
The route passes through
towns and villages
at regular intervals.

RIDE SEASON:
Summer

CONTRIBUTOR/RIDER INFO

Neža Peterca runs What
Happened, a company
that repairs and upcycles
outdoor kits. She is also
the co-founder of Sisters in
the Wild, a community of
women bikepackers. She
was joined for parts of this
ride by friends Katherine
Pierce and Nina Kljun.

SUMMER SOLSTICE TREK IN THE LAURENTIAN MOUNTAINS

→

ROUTE
**THE FORÊT
OUAREAU LOOP**

LOCATION
CANADA

AS BIKEPACKERS, we so often dream of far off places. When the whole world is your oyster, it is sometimes all too easy to overlook the adventure that can be found right outside your front door—especially if that door happens to open out into the middle of the city. Many of us know our local trails and roads intimately. They are our training loops, commuting routes, and midweek escapes. The exploration of our own cities tends to be limited to how far we can ride in a single day or what we naturally encounter during our commutes. But have you ever looked at the map to see what is beyond that invisible boundary? What if you kept on riding a little longer? Where might you end up?

The June sun was already high when Trevor Browne and David Huggins-Daines negotiated the Montreal streets and bike paths, swapping concrete underpasses for tree-lined gravel roads. What better time to adventure from the door than the summer solstice? Daylight stretches out before you like a blank sheet of paper waiting for the first trace of a line. A deadline is only prescribed by the willingness of your legs to resist fading before the light does. The freedom bikepacking brings means you can stop when you drop.

The pair left behind high-rise buildings and then suburbia as they cycled northwestward. The route passes through farmland and forests of maple and birch, eventually picking up the meandering Rivière du Nord into the Forêt Ouareau Regional Park. *Ouareau* means "far away" in Algonquin, a fitting name for a place that is fewer than 100 kilometers (62 miles) from Montreal but feels like a whole different world.

The river acted as a handrail for the rest of their first day, guiding Trevor and David to the perfect camping spot to dip weary toes in crystal-clear water. Feet were not the only things cooled: it seemed churlish not to take advantage of the microbreweries they passed en route and stock up for the evening ahead. The Forêt Ouareau Regional Park campsite is in a secluded, sheltered spot, with pitches nestled between trees, perfect for hanging a hammock and swaying yourself to sleep.

The pair took turns plucking another can of beer from their all-natural cooler nestled between rocks on the river bed, while the other tended to their evening meal. They were in no hurry as the sun finally began to dip in the sky and turn the silvery bark of the birch trees into rich bronze. →

The following day's route took them on the path of least resistance through the surrounding hills, escorted by valleys farther north and west before eventually swinging south. Maybe it was the beers the night before or the sharp bursts of climbing to the high point near Lac Dufresne, but the pair were due for a refueling stop.

Fortunately most of the small towns that the route passes through have a greasy spoon. And every cafe in the area serves poutine, the treasured Quebecois delicacy. Loaded up with fries, gravy, and rubbery cheese curds—there's nothing delicate about that—it was lucky the trail trended downhill the rest of the way.

After shedding some height, David and Trevor hit the P'tit Train du Nord trail, an old railway line repurposed as a cycle way in the summer and a ski trail in the winter. It makes for a speedy, traffic free return toward the outskirts of Montreal.

Re-entry into city life is not always as easy as leaving it. It is amazing how quickly we forget the background noise of traffic. Grid-style streets and endless junctions feel constraining after two days of big skies and sweeping gravel tracks. There is joy to be found in the contrast though. Dirt-encrusted legs welcome the easy pedaling of tarmac and the enforced rests that traffic lights provide. And

because the journey started from the front door, it ends there too. There is no long drive to worry about or flights to miss, but simply a hot shower to step into and a welcoming sofa to recline on.

Perhaps the best thing about a door-step trip is that it captures the sense of adventure and freedom that cycling brought us when we were children. As we grow older, all of us sometimes lose the giddy enthusiasm we had as kids. It is still there though—we just need to work a little harder to let it out. The only difference now is we do not have our parents to tell us to be back in time for dinner. ○

THERE'S SOMETHING ABOUT A DOORSTEP ADVENTURE THAT RECAPTURES OUR CHILDHOOD
DESIRE TO EXPLORE. A CAMPFIRE ONLY ADDS TO THE EXPERIENCE.

KEY TRIP NOTES

REGION/LOCATION(S):
Forêt Ouareau, Quebec,
Montreal

CATEGORY:
Overnighter

DISTANCE:
280 km (174 mi)

TERRAIN:
Quiet country roads,
gravel, and some
rougher doubletrack

SKILL LEVEL:
Intermediate. Non-technical
terrain, but some steep climbs
that may require pushing,
depending on fitness level.

HIGHLIGHTS:
Escaping the city, doorstep
adventure, riverside
camping, and local beers.

**ESSENTIAL
GEAR/EQUIPMENT:**
Camp kit, extra space in
your bags to stow craft
beer sourced from the
microbreweries en route.

RESUPPLY INFO:
Rawdon is perfect for picking
up supplies just before camp.
It has a couple of grocery
stores, a liquor store, and a
hardware shop for fuel. The
route passes through a large
number of towns and villages,
many of which have greasy
spoon cafes serving poutine.

RIDE SEASON:
Spring–Autumn

CONTRIBUTOR/RIDER INFO

Forêt Ouareau Loop is a
280 km (174 mi) overnight
route, devised by David
Huggins-Daines, starting
and finishing in his home
city of Montreal. Trevor
Browne also resides in
Montreal. Together the pair
had ridden sections before,
but wanted to stitch it
together into a grand loop.
The result was perfect for
their annual solstice ride.

HOW TO TRAVEL AS A FAMILY

Melanie and Joachim Rosenlund and their one-year-old daughter, Alva, intrepidly set off on their first multiday off-road adventure together to ride the Rainbow Road into the backcountry of New Zealand's South Island. The family has since gone on to ride more kilometers together, and Alva is now two and a half. Melanie and Joachim unpack their experiences of bikepacking as a young family.

"Big mountains are the place we feel most at home, and we wanted to share the joys of bikepacking and life on the road with Alva," says Joachim. For him, it is key to not let other people's worries become your own. "The noise of everyone telling us how crazy our idea was, was buzzing, but we're glad we overcame that. The privilege of spending 24/7 together as a family outdoors, with nowhere to be and no disturbances from the real world, was worth it. Watching Alva's growth—her confidence and enthusiasm for her natural surroundings—has been a joy!" the both of them agree. It is easy to forget that bikepacking is an escape and challenge for parents too. "The comfort zone is a great place, but nothing grows or sparks there," says Joachim. "Terrains and distances shrink, but as a family it is about being in the great outdoors, and doing our best to make sure Alva doesn't pick poisonous plants."

As an experienced bikepacker himself, Joachim stresses the need to forget anything you know already. "Start with a day ride before taking on an overnighter. Try to figure out what your kids like doing off-bike and try to incorporate [those activities]. Kids are incredibly resilient. As long as you're having a good time, your kids mostly will too—and vice versa. Stop whenever they want; bikepacking is as much about them exploring the surroundings as it is about riding. Having exact daily goals can be counterproductive, and make the most of nap times to cover some ground. Food-wise, plan meals beforehand to make shopping,

cooking, and preparation easier and less time consuming while on the road," says Joachim. For their 134 kilometer (83 mile) Rainbow Road trip, Joachim and Melanie figured it should be doable in five days, which is the typical food and supply carrying capacity for adults. Melanie adds, "Alva was still being breast-fed, so her supply was always 'on board.'" Remember that you will end up with more trash than you usually would, so leave space in your bag. Once you have stopped for the day, turn your tent into a familiar safe space for your children. Find a setup that works and use the same setup every day. However, what worked when your child was one year old probably will not work when they are three. It is a continuous journey.

In terms of carrying kids on a bike, "we used a bike seat that attaches to the stem, so Alva is between my arms," says Joachim. "This particular seat only goes up to three years old or 15 kilograms [33 pounds], so we will be testing a

shotgun seat—an additional saddle between you and the handlebars—as we love the position, but we're not sure how long rides can be like that, as it has no backrest and she needs to hold on all the time." Trailers are the most popular and practical choice for traveling with kids.

"Oh, and mind your language. It is contagious!" ends Joachim. ○

→

GOOD TO KNOW

TYPICAL FAMILY RIDING DAY:
20–50 km at 7 kph
(12–31 mi at 5 mph)

GOLDEN RULES—FAMILY:
● Dial your bike setup for off-road: Bike seat? Shotgun seat? Trailer? Tag along or trailer bike? Their own bike? Try renting/borrowing setups before investing.
● Be realistic with route terrains and distances. Expect regular breaks and plans to change. If remote, carry a SPOT tracker or satellite phone for emergencies. Fancy a challenge? See how many kilometers you can squeeze in during nap times.
● Do not ask your child to live in your bikepacking world; visit their world instead.

THREE THINGS TO TAKE—FAMILY:
● Quality outdoor clothes for kids and a carrier for naps. Try a foldable carrier that packs well
● A robust, roomy tent. Kids will use the mats as a bouncy castle. Look into coupler kits for your sleeping mats to create one big sleep space
● Small, waterproof, and indestructible books

KIDPACKING COTOPAXI: A FAMILY ADVENTURE AROUND AN ACTIVE VOLCANO

———————————————→

LOCATION
**COTOPAXI NATIONAL PARK,
ECUADOR**

THE DAMMER family was still in "farm mode." They rushed to finish chores on their sustainable, organic finca located in the Andes. Marcela wrapped a batch of home-made cheese while Michael collected eggs. Their children—Koru, six, and Antu, 3—were barely able to concentrate on their homeschooling lessons, excited for a more active element coming soon to their curriculum: a bikepacking adventure. Gear for four, including neatly piled clothes, a tent, and sleeping bags, was stacked and spread out on the floor of their home. The children collected together their essential supplies, including a few items rarely seen stuffed in an adult's saddle bag. *The Tale of Peter Rabbit* and a teddy bear smuggled their way in among the usual cooking equipment and GPS devices.

This was not Koru and Antu's first bike adventure. Koru was first towed on a bike trailer for an overnighter when he was five months old and

spent his first birthday in the middle of a 10-day bikepacking trip in the Peruvian Andes. Antu's life has been similarly full of riding. The nomadic lifestyle is equal parts completely normal and wildly exciting to them, something to be looked forward to and enjoyed.

The family's plan was to circumnavigate the mighty Cotopaxi, riding through the national park that surrounds one of the highest active volcanoes in the world. The elegant, conically shaped mountain stands at the center of 400 square kilometers (154 square miles) of volcanic lands that have an almost lunar surface, interspersed by low grasses and scrubby vegetation. Its summit lies at almost 6,000 meters (19,685 feet) above sea level, and massive glaciers dress its flanks, acting as hidden sources to icy springs below. The springs are like oases, their verdant greens and luscious plant life contrasting the brown and gray volcanic colors of the rest of the plateau. →

The Dammers set off, Marcela towing Antu in a trailer, Koru sitting on the back of Michael's long tail cargo bike. Strapped to the usual bikepacking kit were two much smaller bikes: a scoot along for Antu and a pedal bike for Koru. The kids mixed self-propelled travel with enjoying a free ride when they felt like it. But there were far more important tasks, like exploring behind rocks, chasing insects, and splashing in streams in their welly boots. As they rode with their parents, Antu and Koru had other crucial roles to fill.

The Head Wildlife Spotter was always busy noticing wild horses, deer, foxes, and occasionally cattle roaming around the volcanic landscape foraging for vegetation, which reminded the family of vibrant coral reefs. Meanwhile the Snack Manager ensured the family did not go hungry, dishing out homemade fruit leather.

Distances were short, of course, but no less adventurous for it. Camp was made early and broken late. The whole team helped to pitch the tent, collect water from the nearest stream, and prepare dinner. Stories were read and told, and games played. There was always time for a little more exploring before dinner, eking out the last of the fun for the day. With the stars twinkling above them, it rarely took long for the children to doze off, buried deep into sleeping bags, exhausted from a day of endless play and discovery. ○

"THE KIDS MIXED SELF-PROPELLED TRAVEL WITH ENJOYING A FREE RIDE WHEN THEY FELT LIKE IT."

RIVERSIDE BREAKFAST: HOT OATMEAL WITH DRIED FRUIT AND FARM YOGURT.

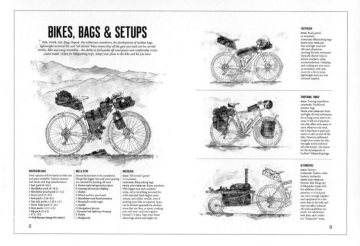

BIKES, BAGS & SETUPS

When it comes to bikepacking, what matters most is the journey and not the destination. Choosing the roads less traveled, connecting to the surroundings every pedal of the way, and embracing the freedom it all offers: long-distance cycling is more than a method of transportation—it's a vibrant traveling philosophy.

Bikepacking presents a roundup of real journeys from all around the world and for all levels of expertise, as told by their protagonists, and gives the reader the lowdown on the tips and tricks to plan their expeditions. Co-edited by expert bikepacker Stefan Amato, this book is an invitation to pack a bag and prep the bike—adventure awaits.

gestalten

ISBN 978-3-96704-013-5

KEY TRIP NOTES

REGION/LOCATION(S):
Cotopaxi National Park

CATEGORY:
Circular loop

DISTANCE:
60 km (37 mi)

TERRAIN:
There are route options to
suit all riders, including well-
packed surfaces wide enough
for trailers to be pulled by a
regular touring bike.

SKILL LEVEL:
Easy–intermediate. Most of
the ride is at altitude above
3,500 meters (11,483 feet).

HIGHLIGHTS:
Taking your time on the trail,
finishing early, and taking
afternoon hikes on terrain
that is not suitable for riding.

**ESSENTIAL
GEAR/EQUIPMENT:**
Everything you need to be
self-sufficient for the duration
of the ride. Camp and cooking
kit, a well-stocked tool kit,
and spares. The weather can
change quickly. Be prepared
with a good onion-style
layering system. If you
are planning a kidpacking
adventure, it is wise to pack
light for yourself to allow
more space for extra layers
for the children. A deck of
cards, books, and a cuddly
friend are mandatory.

RESUPPLY INFO:
Bring food for the entire
route. There are virtually no
resupply options in the park.
Water is readily available.

RIDE SEASON:
June to mid-September

CONTRIBUTOR/RIDER INFO

Michael Dammer and
his wife Marcela live on a
sustainable organic farm in
the Ecuadorian Andes. They
homeschool their children,
Koru and Antu, in between
riding bikes and exploring
the high mountains.

HOW TO TRAVEL SOLO

Following a stint racing bikes professionally and then working as a cycling journalist, Josh Cunningham set off from London one midwinter's morning to ride 21,000 kilometers (13,000 miles) to Hong Kong. The journey gave Josh the "chance to get to know places deeper," while also drawing his attention to "all the in-between places" that are easily missed. Josh helps unpack the key takeaways for riding solo.

The freedom, flexibility, and nimble nature of traveling solo definitely lends itself to both lengthier journeys and the challenge of bikepacking. The fewer the riders, the more focus there is on the riding itself. Following your own schedule, you can ride, eat, sleep, and repeat as freely as you wish—even if you have to carry everything you need yourself. Josh observed that "solo riding forces you out of your bubble and opens up the potential to connect with the world and people around you. Strangers are naturally more hospitable to an individual. Whereas in a group dynamic, what you get in the comfort of existing relationships, you sacrifice in the excitement of new ones." Company has a way of working itself out too. "On a shorter trip, chances are you'll relish the solitude, and escape is definitely one of the pros to riding solo. But without the opportunity for shared experiences, loneliness can definitely roll in quite easily, and motivation has the potential to wane," says Josh. "However, being on your own does boost your willingness to interact or find others to ride with, and the flexibility of bikepacking solo also affords more opportunities to meet and ride with other people."

If you are traveling solo, there are other factors to think about too, including safety and skill level. "Safety is definitely more of a consideration for solo riders, not least because it is you—and only you—making decisions. There is nobody to share the burden of decision-making and logistical-thinking," says Josh. Experience levels count for a lot, both geographically, in terms of challenging terrain, and meteorologically, in terms of climate and weather. As Josh puts it: "Basically, avoid heading anywhere alone unless you know how to get yourself out again." Solo travel, especially as a woman, is less common and has the potential to attract attention with the intrigue and vulnerability that comes with traveling by bike. "Have your wits about you in some scenarios; be trusting in others. Weigh up the risks and trust your instinct," says Josh. If it helps, try to seek a riding partner for sections of your ride you might feel apprehensive about. That said, some aspects of bikepacking are made simpler solo: there are no differences in riding abilities and mindsets to accommodate, and wild camping is more efficient and conspicuous. "You only need one tent or bivvy to set up and keep out of view. For a beginner, I would suggest camping at the first available opportunity near a town, village, or house to be as close to other people as possible without them knowing about it, in case you do need help. Side roads, farm tracks, dead ends, and open gates are all signs of a possible wild camp spot. Think about who might be around later in the evening or early in the morning. Wait until dusk before setting up camp, and be gone early," says Josh.

The hardest thing about a solo bikepacking trip is leaving the front door in the first place. Do not pack your fears; you will not regret it. ○ ⟶

GOOD TO KNOW

TYPICAL SOLO RIDING DAY:
60–150 km at 15 kph
(37–93 mi at 9 mph) over decent terrain

GOLDEN RULES—SOLO:
• Talk to people, be gracious, and say yes
• Have a good idea of your route, rough overnight points to aim for, and Plan Bs. Carry a SPOT (GPS) tracker, or at least let friends and family know where you expect to be, and when
• Look after number one, and two, your bike. Know how to fix basic things to keep you on track.

THREE THINGS TO TAKE—SOLO:
• Paper map, the guaranteed conversation starter
• Book, sketchbook, and journal
• Music, podcasts, and audiobooks

THE CREATION OF A ROUTE: THE BUSHRANGER ESCAPE

ROUTE
THE BUSHRANGER ESCAPE

LOCATION
AUSTRALIA

THE TINY VILLAGE of Walcha Road has a population of 20. Standing outside the heritage-listed railway station, making final adjustments to her bike setup, Jorja Creighton briefly raised that figure to 21. What was once a bustling service stop for the local wool, livestock, and superphosphate industries was now virtually deserted. Pre-ride checks complete, Jorja swung her leg over the bike and set off pedaling, turning her back on the historic town, with a plan to make her return in seven days.

Jorja was in the middle of another recce of the route that would become her Bushranger Escape. She was inspired to create the route after repeated questions from friends and other riders asking for recommended routes or asking where she rode. This was an opportunity to do more than just share a GPS track, but to research, test ride, design, document, and publish a route that would inspire others to discover a new part of Australia. Jorja wanted the Bushranger Escape to be a route that would allow its riders to learn more about the people who thrived, survived, and died in a remote but historic part of the Northern Tablelands of New South Wales.

The end result was a 540-kilometer (336-mile) dirt road loop, jumping off Australia's highest plateau and clambering back up again. It takes in a diverse range of →

KEY TRIP NOTES

REGION/LOCATION(S):
Northern Tablelands
of eastern New South
Wales, Australia

CATEGORY:
Outback exploration.
Multiday circular loop

DISTANCE:
540 km (336 mi)

TERRAIN:
90 percent gravel and
dirt roads, and a small
amount of tarmac

SKILL LEVEL:
Intermediate. The overall
distance, altitude gain, and
remoteness of some of the
route requires a good base
level of fitness, but in good
conditions the riding is on
good terrain.

HIGHLIGHTS:
Climbing and descending
Australia's largest tableland.

**ESSENTIAL GEAR/
EQUIPMENT:**
Camp gear, GPS, and
clothing options to suit
unpredictable weather,
including a waterproof jacket
and some warm layers.

RESUPPLY INFO:
There are two resupply
options on the route.
In Nundle, at the
150-kilometer (93-mile)
mark and in Nowendoc,
at the 440-kilometer
(273-mile) mark.

RIDE SEASON:
This route is rideable all
year round, however, the
shoulder seasons see
the mildest temperatures.
Winter (June and July) can
see temperatures down to
minus 10 degrees Celsius and
snowfall in the higher regions.

CONTRIBUTOR/RIDER INFO

Jorja Creighton, aka Jambi-
Jambi, is based in Australia.
The Bushranger Escape is the
first of a series of routes that
she intends to develop and
make available to the public.

pastureland, pine forest, rainforest, valleys, and mountaintops. But of more interest to Jorja was the human history—from ancient to living—of the area.

The history of the surroundings of Walcha Road date back far beyond the 1800s. It has been the home of the Dunghutti and Anaiwan Aboriginal Australians for tens of thousands of years. The wide, lush, and fertile land has led to the area being known as the "pasture wonderland" by proud locals.

Jorja passed through dozens of forgettable townships, wedged in between valleys. Villages like Niangala, which remain without phone service, are alive with gossip of who slept with who or why that man has buried so many horses. She rode past the 15 scattered houses that made up the conurbation, wondering if they were inhabited or abandoned. Occasionally she would bump into curious locals and tell them stories that were equal parts hearsay and history.

She would share tales like that of Frederick Wordsworth Ward, better known as Captain Thunderbolt, the "bushranger"—highwaymen or outlaws who used the Australian back-country as their refuge—who escaped from the penal colony of Cockatoo Island in Sydney Harbour. He made his way to the Northern Tablelands, robbing properties, mail coaches, and hotels in a seven-year spree that made him the longest-roaming bushranger in Australian history. Eventually he met his demise in a gunfight in 1870. His story has lived on in culture though. There is something very human about the romanticization of outdoor life, regardless of the questionable morality attached.

At that time, thousands of hopeful gold prospectors had flocked to the area in the hope of "fossicking" for their fortune. There are dozens of tales of dirty tactics in the race for riches. On one of her recce loops, Jorja rode just after high rainfall, and the roadside dirt had been washed away to reveal a belt buckle, bullet, pan, and neck of a whisky bottle. These objects were tangible connections to a history only a few generations old.

During her hours and days in the saddle, Jorja gradually panned for nuggets, refining the route, keeping the best parts, and returning to the map where it could be improved. She lived her life as a bikepacking version of a bushranger, swapping theft and robbery for a more philanthropic approach of sharing her trail's gold. ○

FEAR AND FRIENDSHIP
ON THE BAJA DIVIDE

ROUTE
BAJA DIVIDE

LOCATION
**UNITED STATES
AND MEXICO**

JUST BEFORE 8 a.m. on January 2, 2017, Chris Goodman left a small bag containing a T-shirt and a pair of jeans at reception in his downtown San Diego hostel. Attached was a short note saying that he would be back to collect it in nine weeks' time. Then he rolled his bike out onto the street and pedaled down to the waterfront to meet up with 100 strangers.

Nine months before, an open invitation was published to anyone who wanted to join a "group start" and ride the newly created Baja Divide route. Nicholas Carmen and Lael Wilcox had pulled the 2,700-kilometer (1,678-mile) route together in 2016 and wanted to generate some interest when the website went live.

That group had been drawn by tales of beaches and cacti, rich birria and spicy fish tacos, endless dirt trails and epic coastal views. The route connects the Pacific Ocean and the Sea of Cortez, running from San Diego to the very tip of the peninsula. It passes through historic Spanish mission sites lush with shade and water, remote ranchos and fishing villages, bustling highway towns, and every major mountain range in Baja California on miles and miles of beautiful backcountry desert tracks.

Standing at the edge of the group, Chris felt a pang of nerves. Despite his experience, he had never ridden in a big group before, and never in a country where the terrain, culture, →

203

A SANDY DESERT ROAD BETWEEN MISIÓN SAN BORJA AND BAHÍA DE LOS ÀNGELES, WHERE YOU MEET THE SEA OF CORTEZ FOR THE FIRST TIME.

GOLDEN AFTERNOON LIGHT ON THE SEA OF CORTEZ, AND CATCHING A LIFT FROM A LOCAL FISHERMAN
FROM MULEGÉ ACROSS BAHÍA CONCEPCIÓN TO LOS HORNITOS (RIGHT PAGE).

and environment felt such a long way away from the familiarity of Europe. To his surprise, it was the prospect of riding with a group, rather than in the hot Mexican desert, that was the most daunting aspect. It raised self-doubt in his own abilities and anxieties about spending the next two months with strangers.

He did not need to be worried. Over the days and weeks, as the riders progressed south, smaller groups formed. Some sections of trail became unrideable after heavy rain, bikes suffered mechanical problems, and people's natural pace varied. Individuals and packs of riders leapfrogged each other, spreading out and regrouping again in towns, often unexpectedly. This was the beauty of riding in this way. He would spend time with at least four different groups of people, sharing stories while riding, forging

friendships, and enjoying the sense of solidarity that it brought.

There were a few days of solo riding and camping too, which were like relished windows of solitude among the treasured company. The sense of being alone in the wide open desert was humbling and gave time for much appreciated reflection.

It was rarely long before Chris found another group to ride with though. The pattern was always similar. They wild camped and made tacos together. Sometimes they pooled limited and random collections of avocado, peanut butter, tortillas, tomatoes, packets of Tajín seasoning, and their chocolate chip cookie of choice—Chokis—into joint feasts. Mechanical issues were dealt with as a group with knowledge and spares shared freely. And then, when Chris got ill in the desert, those newly formed

friends lent him water and helped him find medical help in the next town.

Back riding, they struggled with Spanish together. They sweated as one up the climbs and grinned from ear to ear at the bottom of roller-coaster descents. Maybe there was sometimes a little too much whooping and hollering for a reserved Englishman, but the group was mostly American, so they were forgiven; it is kind of compulsory, and perhaps even a little bit contagious.

Reflecting on the route, Chris' lasting memories include the scorching, stunning desert, the cacti, and the turquoise seas. But the memories that left a permanent mark on his character are those of a newfound love for riding with others and the joy of sharing a sunrise, sunset, and everything in-between with the same people, living the simplest of lives on the road together. ○

"TALES OF BEACHES AND
CACTI, RICH BIRRIA
AND SPICY FISH TACOS,
ENDLESS DIRT TRAILS AND
EPIC COASTAL VIEWS."

A HOME-COOKED MEAL
PREPARED BY A LOCAL
AT SAN RAFAEL BAY.

BAJA DIVIDE

KEY TRIP NOTES

REGION/LOCATION(S):
Baja Peninsula from San Diego, United States, to San José del Cabo, Mexico
CATEGORY:
Backcountry adventure
DISTANCE:
2,700 km (1,678 mi)
TERRAIN:
95 percent established dirt roads

SKILL LEVEL:
Advanced
HIGHLIGHTS:
Vast desert landscapes, fishing camps, historic Spanish mission towns, and the freshest, tastiest tacos
ESSENTIAL GEAR/EQUIPMENT:
Requires a robust bike with wide tires (recommended 2.6" and above) run tubeless due to the prevalence of cacti thorns. It is advised to travel light in order to leave space for two to three days worth of food and, at times, up to 10 to 12 liters of water. GPS navigation is recommended.

RESUPPLY INFO:
Regular resupply points, but can be sparsely spaced out. Keep an eye on food and water, and stay stocked up.
RIDE SEASON:
November–March

CONTRIBUTOR / RIDER INFO

Chris Goodman left a 20-year career as an environmental consultant to pursue piecing together a life doing what he loves. He is a photographer, writer, bikepacker, mountain bike leader, and drone pilot, among other things.

SOUTH TO SANTA CRUZ: WEST COAST WEEKENDER

KEY TRIP NOTES

REGION/LOCATION(S):
California west coast:
San Francisco to Santa Cruz
CATEGORY:
2–3 day escape

DISTANCE:
200 km (125 mi)
TERRAIN:
Road/gravel
SKILL LEVEL:
Intermediate
HIGHLIGHTS:
Mount Tamalpais sunrises, giant redwood riding and camping, State Route 1 coast roads, state park gravel roads, coastline crab rolls, and Santa Cruz trails, beaches, and cafes
ESSENTIAL GEAR/EQUIPMENT:
Camping kit and water carriers
RESUPPLY INFO:
Mill Valley, San Francisco, Pescadero,

and Half Moon Bay. Once off State Route 1, there is not a lot except for campground stores. Check opening times, but it is worth carrying supplies in.
RIDE SEASON:
Year-round

CONTRIBUTOR / RIDER INFO

The West Coast Weekender was a Pannier.cc production. Joining Paul Errington and Stefan was Erik Mathy, a local Bay Area bikepacker and trail advocate who photographed the trip, and Clayton Wangbichler from Wilderness Trail Bikes.

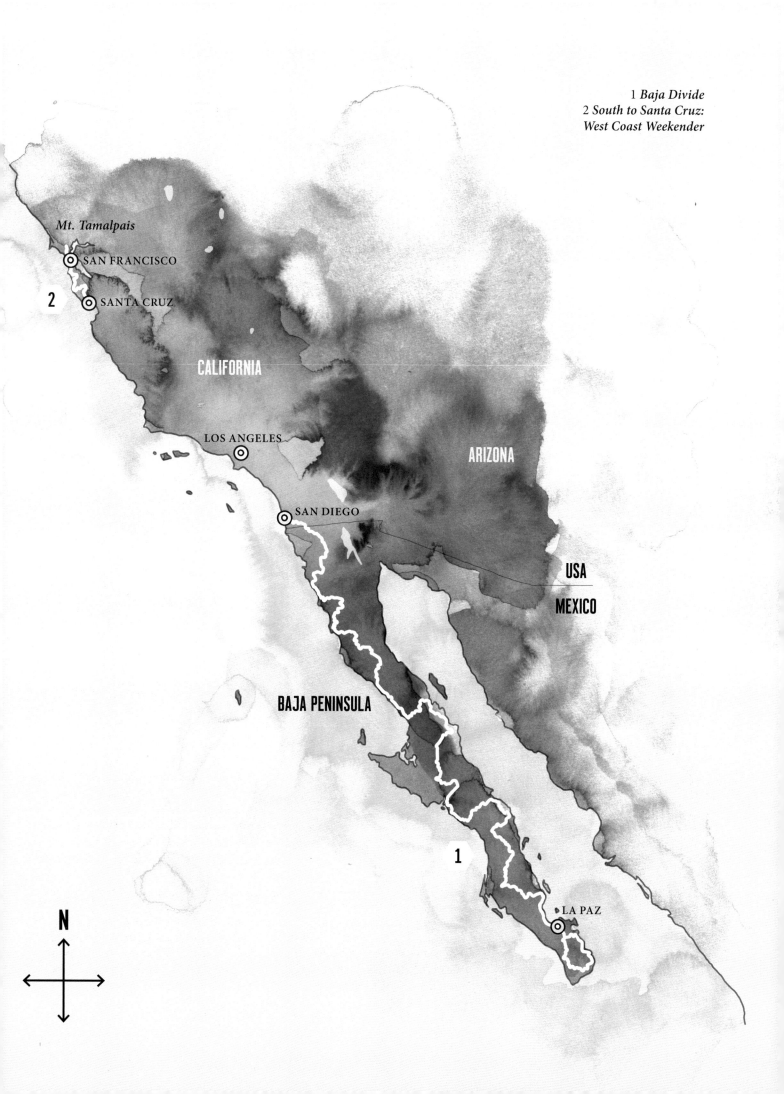

1 *Baja Divide*
2 *South to Santa Cruz:
West Coast Weekender*

Mt. Tamalpais

◎ SAN FRANCISCO

2   ◎ SANTA CRUZ

CALIFORNIA

◎ LOS ANGELES

ARIZONA

◎ SAN DIEGO

USA

MEXICO

BAJA PENINSULA

1

◎ LA PAZ

N

AN OFF-ROAD ADVENTURE ALONG THE NORTH CALIFORNIAN COAST

ROUTE
**SOUTH TO SANTA CRUZ:
WEST COAST WEEKENDER**

LOCATION
UNITED STATES

LOSING YOURSELF IN a map of California is dangerous knowing you only have time for a three-day trip starting and ending in San Francisco. Yosemite, Tahoe, Joshua Tree, and Death Valley are alluring, and look somewhat close to each other on a map. However, in reality, they are spaced far enough apart that each justifies its own bikepacking trip. With all of this in mind, Paul Errington and Stefan's plan was to escape San Francisco and ride 200 kilometers (125 miles) south to Santa Cruz via the Pacific coast roads and trails of the Santa Cruz Mountains. On the first night they would glamp at a ranch tepee site in the hills behind Pigeon Point Light Station Historic Park, the second night they would bivvy out among giant redwoods in Big Basin Redwoods State Park, and then stay at an Airbnb in Santa Cruz on the last night.

Shortly after sunrise coffees high on Mount Tamalpais, overlooking the fog-flooded San Francisco Bay, Paul and Stefan took off on a fun ripper of a descent to Mill Valley. A quick pause for breakfast at a hipster cafe, and the guys were then joining commuters on the Bay cycle paths through Sausalito and over the Golden Gate Bridge, toward the city, before classic San Fran suburban street scenes met the classic Pacific Coast Highway (State Route 1) touring route, where folks with surfboards in arms ran across the sand-sprinkled bike →

DESPITE SAN FRANCISCO'S SIZE, YOU CAN ESCAPE QUICKLY—ESPECIALLY INTO THE MARIN HEADLANDS, OR UP MOUNT TAM.

"STATE PARKS MAKE GREAT, ACCESSIBLE PLAYGROUNDS FOR CYCLISTS AND HIKERS."

lanes to catch the mid-morning surf. Some life here.

The back lanes of Pacifica offered the first chance to head inland, off-road, into the hills on the Old San Pedro Mountain Road toward Half Moon Bay for local beers and crab rolls, before retreating to a ranch tepee at the foot of Butano State Park. The faded pastel hues of the Pacific sunrise were another treat, a view with nothing between the outdoor chiminea and Japan. A hearty huevos rancheros camp breakfast not only felt apt on a ranch, but would also be the fuel to ride up the fire roads from sea level to the high points of the Butano and Big Basin parks. This area forms part of the Santa Cruz Mountains, whose highest peak is Loma Prieta (1,154 meters [3,786 feet]).

NOTE: At this point it is important to mention California's increasing forest fires over the last few years. Since we visited in 2018, unfortunately large areas of these giant redwood forests are now razed to the ground, including the Eagle Rock Lookout Tower high above Big Basin Redwoods State Park. We debated including this story, but it was agreed that acknowledging and highlighting these climate issues was better than erasing them altogether. Year after year, fires remain a big threat across the state.

The redwoods of southern Santa Cruz were first "discovered" during the 1769 Portolá expedition, the first European land entry and explora-

tion of the present-day state of California. However, it was not until the end of the nineteenth century that the trees began to gain international appreciation for their monumental size. The 2,500-year-old trees have reached heights of 100 meters (325 feet) and spanned 15 meters (50 feet) across. Appreciation, however, needed to turn to preservation as San Francisco boomed, and in 1900, the Sempervirens Club formed to protect these old-growth forests from logging. In 1902, the Big Basin Redwoods State Park was the first to be established, and now has the honor of being California's oldest state park. Butano State Park—which is over 4,000 acres of canyons and uplands, some of which Paul and Stefan had just ridden—followed in 1957, along with Castle Rock and Portola. Today, these parks make great, accessible playgrounds for cyclists and hikers.

Nearing Big Basin Redwoods State Park's visitor center, you will start to notice the volume of hikers and the purring of V8 engines. The park's proximity to cities means it can get busy, but early in the year it was not too crowded and the guys were able to pitch up at one of the ride-in camps, which typically have pitches set up, food lockers, and fire pits. In these California State Parks, you will need to book your camping pitch, get a permit, and sign a waiver saying you will be "crumb clean" to stop the jay and raven

population from increasing, which protects the smaller endangered birds. You can head to more remote, no frills camps like Sunset or Lane Trail Camps. Rolling bivvy bags out in the small clearings among giant redwood trees, conversation with neighbors for the night flowed quickly. While the last drops of the bourbon were passed around, the fire died down. Living to daylight hours is definitely one of the simple joys of life on the road.

After camp coffees and a grits breakfast, glimpsing the Eagle Rock Lookout Tower at 758 meters (2,486 feet) was the beacon Paul and Stefan had been aiming for since leaving Mount Tamalpais three days prior. Given its lookout credentials, the 360-degree views are, of course, worth the climb. To the north and west is the Pacific Ocean, merged with the hazy blue skies, and to the east, the Loma Prieta peak loomed. Otherwise it was a blanket of dense forest as far as you could see. From there, the long ride down on Empire Grade tarmac is a well-earned descender's delight. In a flash you will have ridden the 20 kilometers (12 miles) into Santa Cruz, unless, of course, you opt for a detour to ride the vast network of mountain bike trails in the hills above the town, which organizations like Mountain Bikers of Santa Cruz are doing a great job of building, preserving, and promoting. Time to order ceviche on the beach and go for a surf.

Until next time, California. ○

HIGH-ALTITUDE CROSSING FROM COLORADO TO UTAH

→

ROUTE
SAN JUAN HUTPACKING

LOCATION
UNITED STATES

JOSHUA WEINBERG propped up his bike outside a bar in Silverton, Colorado, slotting the front wheel into a bike stand where a hitching post would have stood a century ago. Named after the precious metal found in the surrounding hills, Silverton was originally a gritty mining community embedded deep in the San Juan Mountains of southwestern Colorado. Like many mountain towns, it has evolved and is now a destination for skiers, backpackers, and, of course, mountain bikers. There is no disguising Silverton's history though. Its buildings are weathered and patinated, set back on either side of a dirt road. It still feels a bit like the Wild West out here.

It was from Silverton that Joshua and a small group of riders had come together on a trip organized by San Juan Huts. The soon-to-be friends would spend the next week riding to Moab, Utah. Although the scenery changed—drastically at times—the sense of awe remained the same. The group would gasp for breath while grinding up hill, unaccustomed to whole days spent above 3,000 meters (9,843 feet) altitude. Yet as the week

progressed, their lungs and legs adjusted to the task. And for every climb, there was a glorious descent, sometimes for miles on end, careening down forgotten forest service roads or deserted double-track.

They moved through alpine tundra, dodging afternoon electrical storms. They traversed through huge aspen groves and fertile pastures, only occasionally encountering other people. There would be swim stops to bathe in reservoirs and pristine creeks. There were detours to swashbuckle through primitive and overgrown singletrack before rejoining the dirt road a few kilometers along.

Each day started and ended in the same way, becoming their own separate chapters within a larger story. The San Juan Hut System is a network of near identical private huts along the route. Essentially two trailers joined and set in a fixed location, the huts were comfortably equipped with bunk beds for up to eight people and stocked with sleeping bags, wood stoves, and two-burner gas stoves. Lockers were filled with an assortment of canned and dry foods, and two coolers stuffed with perishables (eggs, bacon, butter,

tortillas, and fresh vegetables) and libations. The huts were more than something to look forward to at the end of a long day. They allowed the group to carry the bare minimum with them. No camp kit or sleeping bag to strap to the bike; instead there was just the joy of riding long distances unburdened. Despite traveling relatively light, the group was always fatigued as they pulled up at the end of each day, ready to refuel and recharge.

In the evenings, people found their natural roles, whether that was cooking for the group or washing up after. After dinner, they would sit on the deck, staring up at skies that felt impossibly full with stars.

There were of course the unique moments that etched themselves into memory a little more firmly than others: an entire day navigating an endless labyrinth of gas-mining two-track, getting caked with pulverized sandstone; the celebratory nip of whiskey at the Colorado-Utah state line; and the glorious last hurrah of a lap of the legendary Kokopelli and Porcupine Rim mountain bike trails, followed by finish line burgers and milkshakes in Moab. ○

"ALTHOUGH THE SCENERY CHANGED—DRASTICALLY AT TIMES—THE SENSE OF AWE REMAINED THE SAME."

FRIENDSHIPS WERE QUICKLY FORMED ON THE TRAIL AND CEMENTED OVER BEERS EACH EVENING.

THE PRIVATE NETWORK OF SAN JUAN HUTS RUNS ALONG THE ROUTE. EACH SLEEPS EIGHT, AND HAD BEEN STOCKED WITH FRESH FOOD FOR THE GROUP.

AS THE WEEK PROGRESSED, THE RIDERS ADAPTED TO THE ALTITUDE, NO LONGER GASPING UP EVERY SMALL CLIMB.

"NO CAMP KIT OR SLEEPING BAG TO STRAP TO THE BIKE; INSTEAD THERE WAS JUST THE JOY OF RIDING LONG DISTANCES UNBURDENED."

KEY TRIP NOTES

REGION/LOCATION(S):
Silverton, Colorado, to
Moab, Utah

CATEGORY:
Semi-supported hut-to-hut
mountain biking trip,
point-to-point

DISTANCE:
350 km (218 mi)

TERRAIN:
Dirt roads with optional
singletrack deviations
between huts

SKILL LEVEL:
Intermediate–advanced.
Much of the route is
conducted at altitude,
requiring a good level of
base fitness. Singletrack
sections require some
mountain bike experience.

HIGHLIGHTS:
A multiday backcountry
trip without the need to
carry a full camp kit.

**ESSENTIAL GEAR/
EQUIPMENT:**
Mountain bike, change of
clothes for evenings, both
waterproof and warm layers,
plus the usual spares and
repair kit you would carry
for a few days away.

RESUPPLY INFO:
When traveling with the
San Juan Hut Systems,
the huts are stocked with
sufficient food for the trip.

RIDE SEASON:
June–October

CONTRIBUTOR/RIDER INFO

Joshua Weinberg lives in
Arizona. He is an occasional
contributor to *The Radavist*.
He undertook the trip with
his friend Steven Smith as
part of a group tour.

WTF? FRIENDSHIP AND COMMUNITY IN THE WILD WEST

→

ROUTE
SKY ISLAND ODYSSEY

LOCATION
UNITED STATES

IN THE SPRING of 2017, the Radical Adventure Riders (RAR) met for the first time. Women, trans, femme, and non-binary bike riders came together for a rugged multiday adventure through the Sonoran Desert as part of the lead up to their inaugural summit later that year. The plan was to create an organization that promotes gender and racial inclusivity and representation within cycling, and to foster community connection.

So what happens when you bring together a group of strangers to ride in the Sky Islands? Magic happens.

If you picture a desert in your mind's eye, you may imagine a dry, dead, and desolate landscape. The Sky Islands region is far from that. Its majestic name comes from the pine and oak woodland-covered mountains that stand proud within the grass lowlands. These tree islands create incredible ecosystems with diverse wildlife, from rare wildflowers to lizards.

The crew rode together, supporting each other as they went. The route twisted its way around the flanks of Mount Wrightson—offering views along the Santa Cruz River Valley and toward Mexico beyond—before the dusty red road zigzagged down granite cliffs covered in lichen to the valley floor.

Days were ferociously hot, often with aggressive winds whipping at legs and faces. Mouths were permanently dry in an attempt to ration water until resupply was possible. Yet as inferno-like as the days could be, the nights were bitterly cold. The desiccated desert air allowed all the day's heat to escape into the crystal-clear night sky.

Friendships formed as the group pedaled together and were solidified in the evenings and during snack stops. Card games, hacky sack, and nature spotting punctuated time in the saddle. A shared notebook was passed around to document thoughts, recipes, songs, →

and ideas—a tangible reminder of the conversations that rose with the warm air.

The group's route passed Baboquivari Peak. This land is originally home to the Tohono O'odham tribe, who regards Baboquivari as the "navel of the world," the most sacred place at the center of their cosmology. The location felt apt for a ride of beginnings: beginnings of friendship, beginnings of connection, beginnings of a new collective.

At times the ride felt like a safari tour as wildlife was everywhere. The Radical Adventure Riders rolled through natural tunnels in the tall grass of savannas, past the contorted shapes of yucca trees. Pronghorn antelopes would nap in the grass and jack rabbits would dart away as the riders approached.

A train of riders riding two abreast would disappear into the distance, laughter and chatter drifting behind them like smoke from a steam train. Each time they rounded a corner,

a new island in the sky would reveal itself. And as their bikes linked each island via dirt roads, they also brought each of the Radical Adventure Riders closer together. A tool for transport became a tool for building a community.

At the end of their Sonoran adventure, on returning to Patagonia, the group had discovered what they already knew: the desert was not a dead and lifeless place. In fact, it was completely the opposite. ○

"SO WHAT HAPPENS WHEN YOU BRING TOGETHER A GROUP OF STRANGERS TO RIDE IN THE SKY ISLANDS? MAGIC HAPPENS."

AT TIMES, THE RIDE FELT LIKE A SAFARI TOUR, WITH WILDLIFE AND FLORA EVERYWHERE. THE GROUP WOULD RECORD THEIR SIGHTINGS IN A NOTEBOOK, ALONGSIDE OTHER MEMORIES OF THE TRIP.

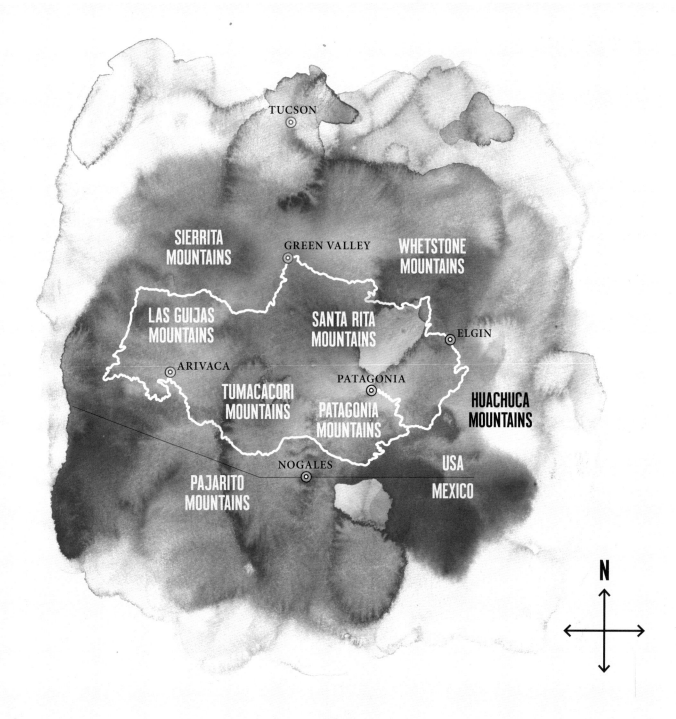

TUCSON

SIERRITA
MOUNTAINS

GREEN VALLEY

WHETSTONE
MOUNTAINS

LAS GUIJAS
MOUNTAINS

SANTA RITA
MOUNTAINS

ELGIN

ARIVACA

PATAGONIA

TUMACACORI
MOUNTAINS

PATAGONIA
MOUNTAINS

HUACHUCA
MOUNTAINS

NOGALES

USA

PAJARITO
MOUNTAINS

MEXICO

N

KEY TRIP NOTES

REGION/LOCATION(S):
Sky Islands region of the Sonoran
Desert, Southern Arizona

CATEGORY:
Circular loop

DISTANCE:
380 km (236 mi) between three
or four days of riding. A shorter
eastern (200 km [125 mi]),
or western (274 km [179 mi])
loop is available.

TERRAIN:
Dirt roads

SKILL LEVEL:
Easy–intermediate

HIGHLIGHTS:
Amazing biodiversity and wildlife

ESSENTIAL GEAR/EQUIPMENT:
GPS device, camping equipment and
cookware, clothes for the drastic change
in temperatures, repair kit, spare tubes,
a battery charger, and some binoculars.
Tires at least 40 mm wide and set up
without tubes are recommended. Call
ahead for permits that are required to
pass through the Appleton-Whittell
Research Ranch (+1-520-455-5522) and
Babacomari Ranch (+1-520-455-5507).

RESUPPLY INFO:
The route passes through a number of
conurbations with fast food restaurants,
small grocers, and gas stations. There

are longer stretches without the
opportunity for resupply. Water is
particularly sparse, so carry plenty
of water storage and a filter.

RIDE SEASON:
November–April

CONTRIBUTOR/RIDER INFO

Sarah Swallow is a co-founder of
the WTF Bikexplorers (now renamed
the Radical Adventure Riders).
She is a contributor to *Thereabouts,
The Radavist, Bikepacking.com,
Lonely Planet,* and other media outlets.
Home is anywhere she pitches her
tent or parks her camper for the night.

OFF ROAD IN
COWBOY COUNTRY

READ ANY ROUTE description of the Oregon Outback trail and you will find warnings of searing summer heat. Brain-melting, dehydrating heat. Yet as Sebastian Hofer and Brady Lawrence rode along the desolate trail, they shook their hands out, trying to force a little blood into their cold, numb extremities as hail and heavy raindrops bounced off the red dirt around them. They had already pulled on every item of clothing they had brought with them, so were grateful to see the faded walls of the Silver Lake Mercantile up ahead, one of the few resupply points en route. The pair sat on the bench outside waiting for the storm to pass and watching the world go by, not that there was a whole lot of life

in the small community of Silver Lake (population: 454) to watch. They knew that riding the trail in mid-September was a bit of a gamble, rolling the dice in the hopes of cooler weather. But this was not quite what they had in mind.

The Oregon Outback is one of the iconic off-road bikepacking routes of the Pacific Northwest in the United States. It winds its way through the stark and beautiful high desert before ending at the Columbia River just across from Washington state. The route is known for its scenic vistas and remote riding through some of the last true areas of cowboy country.

It had rained on and off since Sebastian and Brady started their trip, although they →

RIDING SLIGHTLY OUT OF SEASON, SEBASTIAN AND BRADY EXPERIENCED A DIFFERENT SIDE TO THE USUALLY SEARINGLY HOT OREGON OUTBACK TRAIL.

U.S. POST OFFICE
SHANIKO ORE. 97057

were able to take strategic breaks, like brewing up a coffee under a tree to the percussive soundtrack of rain hitting the dirt, to dodge the worst of the weather. The trail slowly gained elevation as it passed through acres of yellowing farmland, punctuated by towering red pines and cattle gates and their corresponding herds. Up a forgotten forest road, the pair found a secluded creek and fired up the stove to cook some dehydrated dinner before dozing off to the sounds of rushing water.

Ever felt like luck just was not on your side? Day two kicked off with a broken lighter and subsequent cold Quaker Oats breakfast, followed by plummeting temperatures. Around 190 kilometers in (120 miles), the pair decided to book a grimy motel room attached to the Silver Lake Mercantile. They draped their wet clothes over paracord, worsening the smell of the already damp room. Brady laid back on the hotel bed and refreshed his weather app, hoping the forecasted dark clouds would dissipate with a flick of his thumb.

Back on the trail the next day, Sebastian and Brady weaved through towering pines and an ancient lava field embroidered with deep black jagged rocks. Next up was the Red Sauce Trail. It gets its name from the crimson, sandy surface that is known to eat tires and force all but bikers with extra-wide rubber to walk for kilometers. Riding gravel bikes with relatively skinny rubber, the pair knew the day should involve a fair chunk of walking. As they rode, the ground turned from a muddy, slate gray to a deeper and darker red, but the surface never

232

gave way. Finally, a slice of good fortune. The heavy rains had firmed up the red sand and turned the Sauce into a highway.

Cruising through gray hills spotted with pale green sage brush, the weather once again began to shift. In a matter of kilometers, the pair went from riding comfortably in T-shirts to putting on jackets, shells, and gloves. Almost at their breaking point, they decided that maybe you have to make your own luck. Brady called his buddy Dakota and arranged for a lift to Bend, Oregon, for hot showers

and huge bowls of steaming hot pho.

Sitting there, with a belly full of hot broth, they once again checked the forecast and were finally granted nothing but sunshine. The next morning Dakota dropped them off and they grinned at each other as they started the long climb out of the town of Prineville, sunshine warming their shoulders. With the best of the route yet to come, including iconic views of the colossal Mount Adams and Mount Hood volcanoes, they knew their luck had finally turned for good. ○

LIFE IS ALWAYS BETTER AFTER A COFFEE BREWED ON THE TRAIL.

"THE OREGON OUTBACK IS ONE OF THE ICONIC OFF-ROAD BIKEPACKING ROUTES OF THE PACIFIC NORTHWEST."

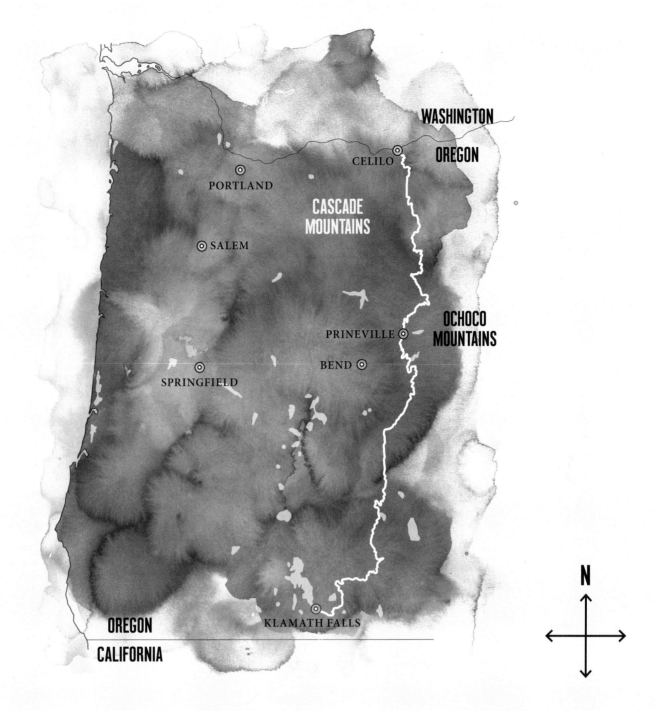

WASHINGTON

OREGON

CELILO

PORTLAND

CASCADE
MOUNTAINS

SALEM

OCHOCO
MOUNTAINS

PRINEVILLE

BEND

SPRINGFIELD

OREGON

CALIFORNIA

KLAMATH FALLS

N

KEY TRIP NOTES

REGION/LOCATION(S):
Oregon. Starts near the California border at Klamath Falls and finishes at the Washington border at Deschutes River State Recreation Area.

CATEGORY:
Point-to-point

DISTANCE:
580 km (360 mi), usually undertaken in five to seven days.

TERRAIN:
Dirt roads, with a couple of rougher sections

SKILL LEVEL:
Advanced. Challenging route, requiring good fitness. Additional challenges around managing water

HIGHLIGHTS:
Remote and desolate landscapes

ESSENTIAL GEAR/EQUIPMENT:
Camp kit, water filter, GPS, clothing for the extremes of temperatures. Be aware that desert nights can get chilly, even in summer.

RESUPPLY INFO:
Resupply and water are extremely limited along the route. There are several sections of longer than 80 km (50 mi) without reliable water resupply, especially in late summer and autumn. Do stop at the Cowboy Dinner Tree (200 km [124 mi]) for steak, but be prepared for big gaps between small town convenience stores.

RIDE SEASON:
Spring and early autumn are ideal. Summer is extremely hot, and winter brings snow to the mountains.

CONTRIBUTOR/RIDER INFO

Sebastian Hofer is a photographer from Hamburg, Germany. Brady Lawrence is a filmmaker from Seattle, United States. The pair are friends who have bikepacked in locations around the world together, although seem to have a knack of attracting bad weather.

RIDING TO THE EDGE OF THE WORLD

ROUTE
HAIDA GWAII

LOCATION
CANADA

HAVE YOU EVER planned a trip only to find that once you arrive at your destination, your original plans were average at best? Not because they were terrible ideas on their own, but because the place offers you an experience beyond your wildest dreams? Ben Johnson's two-week bikepacking tour of Haida Gwaii was one of those trips.

The archipelago of Haida Gwaii, located off the northern Pacific coast of British Columbia in Canada, is an outdoor enthusiast's paradise, from lush rainforests to ancient Haida villages, sandy beaches to crystal-clear lakes.

When seasoned travelers Adam and Frankie Foss (plus Betsy, the tandem bike) joined Ben and

ventured to the remote island, it did not take them long to feel like they were a part of it. Like a pathway engulfed by moss, they felt overtaken by their surroundings. Rather than fighting its pull, they tossed aside their original plans and surrendered to the land, allowing the rhythm of the tide, the direction of the wind, and the ways of Haida Nation to determine their trip.

The trio settled into their first camp at Agate Beach in Naikoon Provincial Park for a few days. Here, the rhythm of life was simple, but the scenery was anything but. They filled their time searching for agates (because it is in the name) on short rides and fleeing rapidly chasing tides. The brightly →

237

ONE OF THE MANY SHIPWRECKS ON THE COAST OF HAIDA GWAII.

"LIKE A PATHWAY
ENGULFED BY
MOSS, THEY FELT
OVERTAKEN BY THEIR
SURROUNDINGS."

OUR FIRST CRAB CAUGHT BY DIP NET!
AGATE BEACH, HAIDA GWAII.

colored gems proved elusive, but night after night the bikers were treated to epic sunsets that more than satiated their desire for vibrant shades.

Next up was a trip to Bonanza Beach. This would involve some serious climbing. Getting started uphill is hard enough on a standard bike, so you can only imagine how difficult it is on a fully loaded tandem. Sweating and subsisting on a diet of cheese and pepperoni, the climb took a while to pass. When it finally did, the group let out howls as they freewheeled. Those howls quickly turned into shrieks as Adam and Frankie discovered how ineffective Betsy's brakes were. Still, as the light of the day faded, they finally rolled into Bonanza Beach and gave each other high fives. Packing enough food for several days away from civilization is always a bit of a challenge. To make

sure they had their bases covered, the ever-resourceful threesome had thought to bring a fishing net. They figured they could bring less food on the bike and fill the gap by dip-netting for crab. It was potentially a risky strategy, but they were sure that luck would be on their side.

The key to catching crabs is to walk out to the tidal flats during the lowest tide of the day, ideally, in a spot where the water is calm. Then, set your eyes on a crab scurrying beneath the surface and strike! At Bonanza, the hungry group found hundreds of baby Dungeness crabs, but no adults, until out of nowhere Adam spotted an adult red rock scramble out of the sand. The chase was on! Using the abundance of driftwood found on the beach, the group made a roaring fire and cooked the bounty just meters away from where

they had caught it. There is something special about sharing a meal in the wilderness with food from the land.

The rest of their time on the island was filled with similar lows and highs. A borrowed boat led to horsefly bites but also a relaxing day fishing and the perfect camp spot at the side of a lake. Five minute hellos with strangers became hour-long, or more, conversations. Plans were made, tweaked, and shelved.

The trio soon discovered that many people come to visit Haida Gwaii for two weeks and never leave. This was not lost on them. They felt so enveloped by the island that they began to consider it for themselves. What if they just left it all behind and lived on the edge of the world, allowing this island to overtake them even more than it already had? ○

DIP-NETTING FOR CRABS AT BONANZA BEACH. THE CATCH: RED ROCK CRABS.

KEY TRIP NOTES

REGION/LOCATION(S):
Haida Gwaii is an archipelago of islands off the coast of British Columbia, Canada.

CATEGORY:
Cycle tour, unplanned adventure

DISTANCE:
240 km (149 mi)

TERRAIN:
Dirt roads and tarmac

SKILL LEVEL:
Easy, although there are some steep climbs that might require pushing.

HIGHLIGHTS:
Settling into a different pace of life, friendly locals, and fresh crab cooked on the beach.

ESSENTIAL GEAR/ EQUIPMENT:
Camp kit, stove, fishing net (and license), and an open mind.

RESUPPLY INFO:
Plenty of opportunities for resupply in towns and villages. Take sufficient food if you head farther into the wilderness.

RIDE SEASON:
Summer

CONTRIBUTOR/RIDER INFO

Coming from a design and digital media production background, Ben Johnson has a curiosity for the unknown and a penchant for exploration. He undertook this journey with his friends Adam and Frankie Foss.

RIDING THE TRANSAMERICA (DIRT ROAD) TRAIL

ROUTE
TRANSAMERICA TRAIL

LOCATION
UNITED STATES

WHEN MOST people imagine the Trans-America Trail (TAT), they picture the classic Adventure Cycling Association route that follows paved roads from Astoria, Oregon, to Yorktown, Virginia. Tom and Sarah Swallow stumbled upon this route while exploring the twisty rhododendron-lined gravel roads of North Carolina and Tennessee. They saw an information board for an off-road motorbike TransAmerica Trail, developed in 1996. They had both always wanted to ride across America. Maybe this route could be the answer to their ultimate cross-country bikepacking quest?

They set off on August 1, 2015, and and rode the TAT over the course of three months. They turned their backs on the Atlantic Ocean and left the outer banks of North Carolina, traveling west over the Great Smoky Mountains. The route followed the back roads of the lush, humid river valleys and forests of southern Tennessee and northern Mississippi. They traveled over the Mississippi River and into the rugged Ozark Mountains in Arkansas before beginning a gradual, straight ascent through the prairie grasslands of northern Oklahoma and the Oklahoma Panhandle. For 170 kilometers (106 miles), the route progressed through northeast New Mexico before navigating northwest into the Rocky Mountains and →

THE RHYTHM OF LIFE IN
THE SADDLE. DAYS BLURRED
INTO ONE, BUT EACH HAD
ITS DISTINCT MOMENTS.

over the high alpine passes of the San Juan Mountains of Colorado. The red rocks of the Utah city Moab were the ride's introduction to a long stretch across the state's high desert, the Great Basin of Nevada, and eastern Oregon.

Tom and Sarah followed the footsteps of the early pioneers of the California Gold Rush as their route finally left the desert and dropped them into the greener land of Surprise Valley, California, and over the Cascade Mountains of Oregon, where water began to flow in the creek beds again. In October, the pair reached Battle Rock Beach in the moody coastal town of Port Orford, Oregon. After three months of navigating the great landmass of the United States, they

finally saw sea again, this time the Pacific stretching far beyond the horizon. Yet somehow this was not the end of something. It was just the beginning.

The TAT was the pair's first bike tour of this scale, and they stumbled their way through. They ran out of water, got stuck in the mud, hid from thunderstorms, slept with bed bugs, and rode with a crosswind for over 1,000 kilometers (621 miles). They did without, snuck water from private property, pushed bikes for kilometers, and sprinted from aggressive dogs. The pair were repeatedly awestruck by the natural beauty unfolding in front of them. Food tasted better than it ever had, sleep felt better than ever,

and encounters with humans were true and honest. It was rewarding. They did hard things and they felt better for it. All of their senses and emotions were heightened, and eventually they found a natural rhythm, pace, and ease of living on the TAT.

It is impossible to condense three months of living in the saddle into a single story. What was meant to be a sabbatical from running a bike shop became so much more. The Swallows realized that they should continue the journey they started with the TAT, navigating the course of life by bicycle and learning as they traveled. On returning home, they sold their bike shop and chose a life on the road. ○

NEW YORK CITY ◉

WASHINGTON DC ◉

TENNESSEE

NORTH CAROLINA

NASHVILLE ◉

CHARLOTTE ◉

◉ CAPE LOOKOUT

ATLANTA ◉

MISSISSIPPI

TRANSAMERICA TRAIL

←————————

KEY TRIP NOTES

REGION/LOCATION(S):
An east-west crossing of the United States, starting in North Carolina and finishing on the Oregon coast.

CATEGORY:
Epic point-to-point, crossing a country

DISTANCE:
8,490 km (5,275 mi)

TERRAIN:
Dirt roads, gravel, jeep tracks, forest roads, abandoned railroad grades, and farm roads. There are also plenty of opportunities for singletrack alternatives along the route.

SKILL LEVEL:
Advanced. Best suited to those with prior bikepacking experience.

HIGHLIGHTS:
The variety of terrain, culture, and time for reflection that crossing a country brings. It is a life-changing experience.

ESSENTIAL GEAR/EQUIPMENT:
A bike suitable for off-road riding: a gravel bike or mountain bike is perfect. GPS device, water storage and filter, camping equipment, cookware, clothes for the change in climates, repair kit and spare tubes, extra battery charger, and most importantly, time. A route of this length will take a couple of months to complete.

RESUPPLY INFO:
As you go farther west, the route becomes more challenging and remote with fewer towns. The maximum distance between towns is around 260 km (162 mi).

RIDE SEASON:
Best started between May and August

CONTRIBUTOR/RIDER INFO

Sarah and Tom Swallow are the former owners of Swallow Bicycle Works. Riding the TAT inspired them to pursue a life of adventure by bike.

UP HIGH IN THE ATLAS

ROUTE
**CIRCUMNAVIGATING
THE ATLAS MOUNTAINS**

LOCATION
MOROCCO

THE FIRST DAY of a long trip is often one of opposites. The stress of rebuilding bikes after a plane trip, sourcing that vital forgotten item, and stocking up on food supplies for the first leg of riding is then followed by the contrasting relief of setting off and the sense of freedom it brings.

It was after noon when Stefan Schott, Stefan Haehnel, and Max Baginski finally escaped the maze of narrow alleys of Marrakech. Dust and spices filled the air and each street swarmed with tourists and street vendors, tightly packed, noisy, and dizzying. When they eventually broke free of the city's clutches they made rapid progress. Fifty flat kilometers (31 miles) passed as quickly as fully loaded bikes allow, and they soon reached the foot of the Atlas Mountains. Any sense of pace quickly dissipated as they winched the first of many steep climbs. Eight hundred kilometers (497 miles) and 12,000 meters (39,370 feet) of climbing lay ahead of them, and despite only being 4:30 p. m., the sun was beginning to set. Resigned to the fact that they would not make their planned mileage that day, the trio found a suitable spot to make camp, build a campfire, and cook dinner as the growing darkness hid the mountains from view for the evening. Out of sight, but not out of mind. They knew the true challenges still lay ahead. →

THERE WERE TIMES THAT IT WAS HARD TO TELL WHERE A VILLAGE ENDED AND LANDSCAPE BEGAN,
AS HOUSES WERE TUCKED INTO EVERY NOOK AND IMPROBABLY SMALL FLAT SPOT.

THE CAMOUFLAGED BUILDINGS WERE BROKEN UP BY A RAINBOW
OF RUGS AND BLANKETS HANGING TO DRY ON THEIR WALLS.

"THEY PASSED THROUGH VILLAGES BUILT FROM THE SAME RED CLAY AS THE PATHS THEY TRUDGED THROUGH."

Day two. Crazy distances still to come, and the three riders were walking rather than pedaling, pushing their bikes up loose, rocky paths. From the comfort of their homes, 100 kilometers (62 miles) a day seemed like a modest target, yet as dusk settled once again, they had covered only 40 kilometers (25 miles) for the day and just 97 kilometers (60 miles) in total. It was hard to stop self-doubt from creeping in. Had they been stupid and naive? As they pushed, they passed through villages built from the same red clay as the paths they trudged through. Small homes were stacked on top of each other, like giant stairs up the mountainside.

Blessed tarmac brought some speed, but also traffic. Facing close passes and moments of chaos as the trio climbed farther on the Tizi n'Tichka Pass, they finally descended the serpentine road to the southern side of the Atlas range, looking out across the endless Sahara Desert.

Following the edge of the range, the two Stefans and Max rode northeast along the National Route 10 highway, dubbed the "Moroccan Route 66." It was an opportunity to drop heads and press on pedals, as they passed stalls selling brightly colored fruit and vegetables.

The wall of the Atlas remained on their left, goading them. It would need to be crossed once more before they could return to Marrakech. The Dadès Gorge climbs steadily for 70 kilometers (44 miles), set deep into the mountains with high cliffs on either side, a slot of daylight directly above. Eventually the riders topped out on the high plateau of the Altas, the thin air at 3,000 meters (9,843 feet) above sea level literally taking their breath away, and the minus two-degrees-Celsius temperature whipping heat away from sweaty backs.

The camouflaged buildings they passed were broken up by brightly colored doors and a rainbow of rugs and blankets hanging to dry on their walls. The locals were always curious and always friendly. Every stop for water or food would bring all the children of the village out to marvel at the group's bikes and kit, each overjoyed with the gift of a sticker.

Leaving the mountains on the penultimate day brought with it a change in landscape as the arid hills gave way to forests and agriculture. The small matter of 170 kilometers (106 miles) and a headwind was all that stood between the riders and their flight home. The practicalities of life began to creep back into their consciousness—a heavier weight to carry than their panniers. The intense oranges of the setting sun lit the city's red walls as they approached. ○

MILAGE WAS HARD WON AND SLOW GOING AS THE GROUP CROSSED THE HIGH ATLAS. FORTUNATELY THE REST OF THE ROUTE REBALANCED THE HIKE/BIKE RATIO.

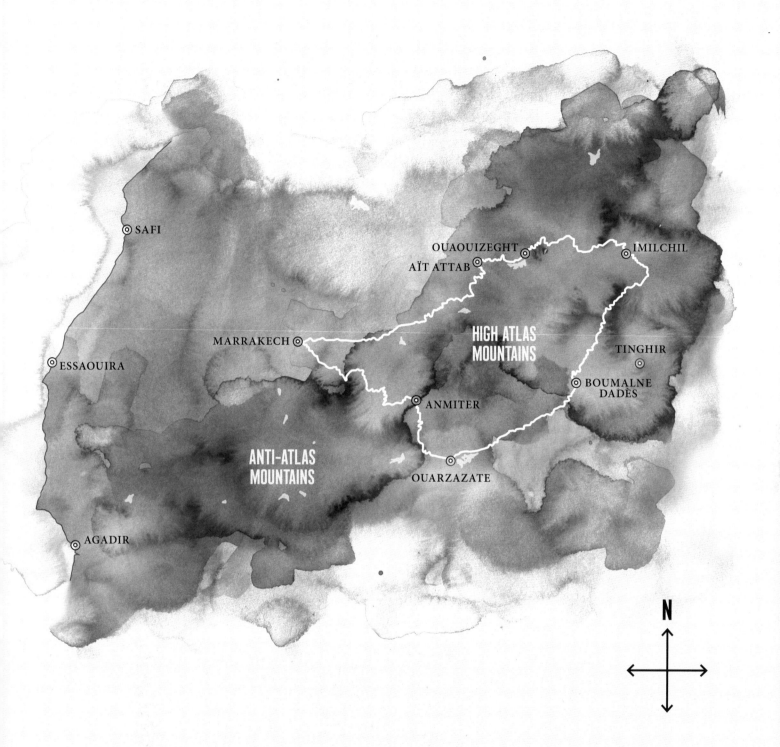

SAFI

OUAOUIZEGHT

AÏT ATTAB

IMILCHIL

MARRAKECH

HIGH ATLAS
MOUNTAINS

TINGHIR

ESSAOUIRA

BOUMALNE
DADÈS

ANMITER

ANTI-ATLAS
MOUNTAINS

OUARZAZATE

AGADIR

N

KEY TRIP NOTES

REGION/LOCATION(S):
Atlas Mountains, Morocco

CATEGORY:
Circular loop

DISTANCE:
840 km (522 mi)

TERRAIN:
Dirt roads, gravel paths, and tarmac

SKILL LEVEL:
Intermediate. Steep terrain and some
hike-a-bike/pushing. Some remote

riding and limited options for shortcuts

HIGHLIGHTS:
Remote mountain landscapes and
friendly welcomes

ESSENTIAL GEAR/EQUIPMENT:
Camp kit (note that it can be
challenging to find fuel for camping
stoves), clothing to cope with extremes
of temperatures, and cycling shoes
suitable for some hike-a-bike.

RESUPPLY INFO:
The route passes through many towns
and villages.

RIDE SEASON:
Northern Hemisphere winter

CONTRIBUTOR/RIDER INFO

Max Baginski, Stefan Schott, and Stefan
Haehnel rode this route in 2015. The
trio chose the Atlas Mountains to follow
up similarly ambitious adventures,
including crossing the Alps on fixed gear
bikes, riding from Berlin to Prague only
checking a map twice a day, and riding
to Poland to climb its highest peak.

HOW TO TRAVEL AS A COUPLE

Matty Waudby and his partner, Clare Nattress, embarked on a year-long series of trips together riding bikes off the beaten track in Norway, Spain, Australasia, and Nepal. Based in the United Kingdom, before their big trip they had only ever ventured out on weekend overnighters together in the Peak District and North York Moors National Park. Matty and Clare share their secrets on bikepacking as a couple.

"Our goals are to have fun, see places, and climb mountains together," says Matty. With a life around bikes, he, and now Clare, believe the bikepacking way of life is the best formula for reaching these goals together. Matty goes on, "life is simple when adventuring by bike. All you have to worry about is food, water, and where you're going to sleep—slow travel at its finest." Clare loves the active travel aspect, and points out how bikepacking as a couple gave her the confidence to take on more challenging routes. "As a beginner, I wouldn't have had the confidence to venture to the start of the Annapurna Circuit alone, let alone wild camp in many of the locations we did," says Clare. "Bikepacking as a couple lowered my guard and made these ace experiences possible. With hindsight, I could've done the same trips without Matty, but would I have had the motivation, or enjoyed them as much?" The chance to bounce ideas and plans is invaluable.

Spending every moment together for a year is definitely a good test of a relationship. If you can bikepack

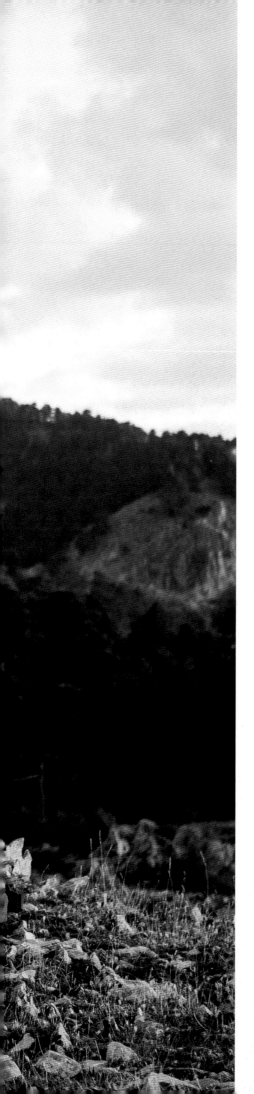

together, you can do anything together, and a shared mindset is pivotal to this. The more days on the road together, the more Matty and Clare got to know what routes suited them best. "In the beginning I was a bit overeager with my route planning, seeking out all the wildest terrain, but facing those challenges every day is pretty unrealistic. Compromise is paramount. Keeping lowish expectations on distance, especially given off-road terrain, allows you to have the experiences you want. For us, bikepacking is about slow travel, soaking in the sights, shooting photos, and enjoying afternoon breaks and beers," they both say.

Matty loves kit, so the practicalities of planning for two were really exciting. "Things like having a double sleeping mat and quilt allowed us to share the load and save a lot of weight. To carry [the gear for] the same comfort level solo would definitely mean heavier bikes," says Matty. Given the potential for spending 24 hours cooped up under canvas if the weather is bad, "don't underestimate the importance of a roomy, strong, discrete, and lightweight tent, as having some personal space is essential," says Matty. It is well worth planning a night in fixed accommodations for a recoup and home comforts every other night, or at least every now and again."

Before heading out, Clare and Matty discussed who would take on what tasks throughout the trip to save time on the road and prevent potential arguments. "Designated roles pre-trip, and on the road, were really important for efficiency and using each other's strengths," says Clare. "For example, each night when we stopped I would prepare the food and cook, while Matty would pitch the tent, inflate the camp mats, and lay out the quilt. It was also a lot easier to avoid arguing!" Riding as a couple is also a challenge. A bit of distance is not a bad thing and nothing should be forced; ride at your own paces as much as possible. Personal space is key off the bike too. Clare admits, "it was important to have general downtime and tent time, as well as separation upon reaching towns and cities on longer trips. I would often visit things like art galleries, while Matty would explore with his camera." ○

GOOD TO KNOW

TYPICAL COUPLES RIDING DAY:
30–100 km at 10 kph
(19–62 mi at 6 mph) over decent terrain

GOLDEN RULES—COUPLES:
● Mindsets must match. Never go to sleep upset or frustrated—any issues will just fester.
● Roles. Designate roles pre-trip to make routines more efficient and avoid getting on each other's nerves while on the road.
● Personal space: both riding and off the bike

THREE THINGS TO TAKE—COUPLES:
● Empathy, and a sense of humor
● A camera, to document your adventures together
● A roomy lightweight tent (look at ways to double-up on sleeping kit) and books, e-books, sketchbooks, and journals

A TIBETAN ADVENTURE

→

ROUTE
SICHUAN KHAM TOURING

LOCATION
TIBET

THE SUN WAS setting as Ed and Marion Shoote set up camp near the edge of the monks' quarters, which was situated on a small hill above the huge monastery of Yarchen Gar. They collected water from one of the standpipes. The temperature was already well below freezing, so the taps were left running overnight. It took a long time to cook at this altitude. The fuel does not burn as efficiently and the boiling point gets cooler the higher you get, so you need to leave it longer to kill the bugs. Earlier on the trip they had discovered that near 5,000 meters (16,404 feet) the MSR stove struggled to burn petrol with the much more limited atmospheric oxygen around. Here, it was working adequately enough.

The couple were in the middle of a 1,500-kilometer (923-mile) tour of the Tibetan province of Kham, now an area claimed by China. Setting off from Kangding, they rode the Sichuan-Tibet Highway and over the Cho La pass to Yarchen Gar before returning to Kangding via back roads.

Just as Ed slipped some noodles in the pan, a kind monk came over and offered them a place to sleep. The thought of a warm, condensation-free shelter was too attractive to decline.

The pair carried their kit over to the monk's place. Behind a gate was a small overgrown yard. His basic house was two rooms with a meditation "cube" on the roof. It was very snug and well insulated, with cloth shoved in every crack.

They sat with the monk for a while and he handed Ed two picture cards—in the style of baseball cards—of the monastery's two main Lamas. He then gifted them an old, worn antique ceremonial dagger. It was maybe eight centimeters high (three inches) with a face on the handle. Humbled by the gift, the pair hunted in their bags for something to give in return. All they had was a large pomegranate. The monk seemed perplexed, but pleased.

The pair slept well in the beautiful room, every inch covered by brightly colored silks. The monk popped his head through the window on his way to morning prayers to check all was OK and then left them in the house. They never saw him again. This temporary, fleeting friendship would last long in their memories though. It typified the pair's time in Tibet. Even as the landscapes and riding became harder and more brutal, the locals remained warm, welcoming, and endlessly generous. →

TIBETAN MOMOS FOR
BREAKFAST IN GARZÊ
AND CLIMBING THE
NEVER-ENDING TRO LA
PASS AT 5050 METERS
(16,568 FEET).

"THE 22 DAYS ON THE ROAD WERE FILLED WITH SHARED MEALS, ACTS OF GENEROSITY, AND PASSING CONNECTIONS."

A few days later, Ed and Marion were getting tired and needed somewhere to sleep. There was no real flat land in the valley to camp and the villages seemed pretty quiet. Eventually they saw a big sign in Tibetan and Chinese pointing up a small track. If they bothered putting a sign up there must be something there? At the top they discovered the Chinese had built a Tibetan village in the middle of nowhere. Small, well-surfaced, and well-lit streets led to modern houses built in the traditional style. They had then resettled some Tibetans there. However, there were yaks and wild dogs all over the place with the associated mess—not ideal for camping. The clean, sanitized model village was not all going to plan, but it seemed the Tibetans had some nice new houses to live in. The riders met a friendly local and asked about sleeping in the village. They were taken to the biggest building of all. After a mobile phone call, another guy turned up and opened the doors. There was an unfinished fancy hotel inside. The vast unfurnished marble floors were covered in an odd yellow dust and some off-cuts of stone, and cables lay about. The pair left their bikes in a room downstairs and were led to a bedless bedroom on the first floor with an en suite bathroom completed, but with no electricity or water.

After showing the local their sleeping mats and bags, the guy let them stay for free and even left them a room key. They cooked outside, and as they sat, his wife delivered a car battery and light to use in the room.

This strange village epitomized their experience, traveling through a disputed land. Regardless of the machinations of authority, the local people found a way to exist, and did so with a warmth and friendliness that belied some of the more sinister threats to their way of life. The couple's 22 days on the road were filled with shared meals, acts of generosity, and passing connections.

Not long after Ed and Marion left, the Chinese authorities drastically cut the size of the Yarchen Gar monastery. It is a stark reminder that despite their resilience, the Tibetan locals still face immense challenges to their culture and way of life. ○

A DETOUR TO A MONASTERY IN THE HILLS NEAR LITANG.

DESCENDING THE TRO LA PASS: A CHINESE TUNNEL HAS SINCE OPENED, BUT TRUCKS STILL USE THE HIGH ROAD.

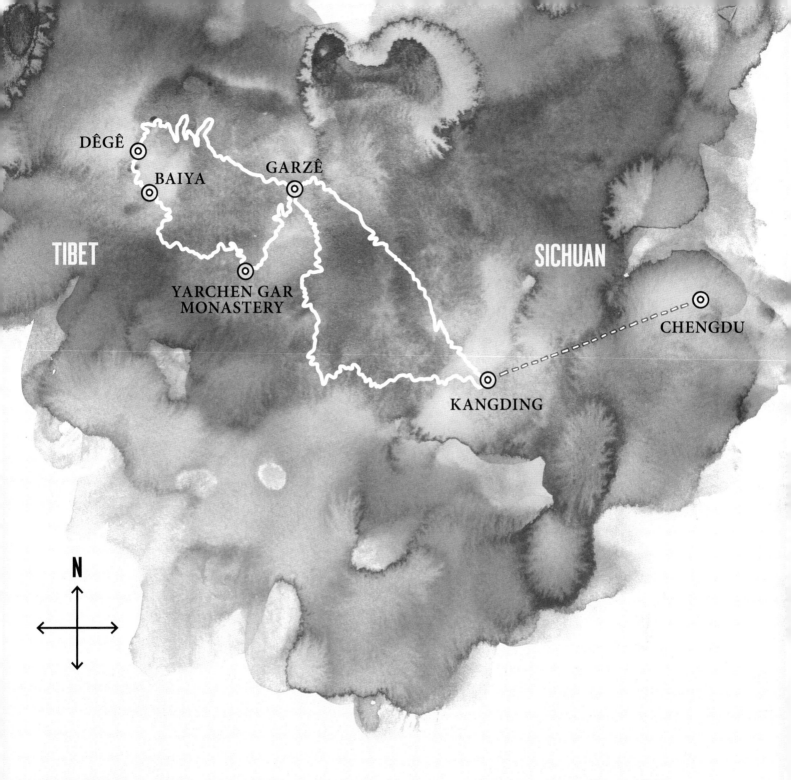

DÊGÊ

BAIYA

GARZÊ

TIBET

YARCHEN GAR
MONASTERY

SICHUAN

CHENGDU

KANGDING

N

KEY TRIP NOTES

REGION/LOCATION(S):
The route passes through the Garzê
Tibetan Autonomous Prefecture,
known as the Kham region of Tibet.
This is a disputed area that China
claims as part of Western Sichuan.

CATEGORY:
Epic adventure

DISTANCE:
1,500 km (923 mi)

TERRAIN:
Mostly tarmac and well-made
dirt roads

SKILL LEVEL:
Advanced. Almost all the route is
above 3,800 meters (12,467 feet)
altitude and it reaches a high point
of 5,050 meters (16,568 feet). This is
high enough for serious issues if you
are not acclimated and makes even the
slightest of climbs tiring, even when
you aren't. There is a total of 16,000
meters (52,493 feet) of altitude gain.
A route best saved for the fittest, but
shorter variations are possible.

HIGHLIGHTS:
Friendly locals and (literally)
breathtaking views

ESSENTIAL GEAR/EQUIPMENT:
Camp gear, tent, sleeping bag, and mat
that are warm enough for sub-zero
nights, and plenty of warm layers.

RESUPPLY INFO:
The route passes through lots of villages
where supplies can be stocked up.

RIDE SEASON:
April–October

CONTRIBUTOR/RIDER INFO

Ed and Marion Shoote live in the Tweed
Valley, Scotland. They have ridden in
over 50 countries around the world.

A SELF-SUPPORTED TRAVERSE OF ICELAND'S INTERIOR

→

ROUTE
ICELAND TRAVERSE

LOCATION
ICELAND

THE GROUP STOOD at the edge of the glacial meltwater river. The frigid water rushed by, rocks occasionally clanking below the surface. The riders—Emily Batty, Adam Morka, Chris Burkard, and Eric Batty—were at almost the exact geographic center of Iceland, surrounded by volcanic peaks and lunar landscapes. For all the sense of adventure that riding brings, it is not often that we reach truly remote locations by bike. Four hundred (249 miles) and four days into their trip, however, the group was completely isolated. Now, they faced a decision: cross the torrent here, or retrace their tracks and take a detour that would add a day to an already epic trip. The river was impassable a week ago. But now in the early morning, and after several days of cold weather with the sun yet to hit the Hofsjökull glacier, the flow was less powerful as much of the water was still frozen from the previous night. The group tentatively threw rocks to judge the depth, and eventually waded across one by one.

The landscape of Iceland is defined by contrasts. The heart of the island feels a world apart from the ragged coastline. Not long after leaving behind the rugged shores and the

bright orange lighthouse of Dalatangi, the foursome traversed the sides of fjords and proceeded through the verdant greens of Hallormsstaðaskógur forest. As they climbed with their backs to the sea at the end of the first day, gaining 1,800 meters (5,906 feet), they left behind a multicoloured world and entered one characterized by the grays and blacks of volcanic rock. There is incredible beauty in the bleakness, but also a lot of empty space. Empty space and empty time—hours of time to ponder while doing battle with a headwind and a track that seems to stretch into eternity.

There are no towns, no villages, no permanent human life in the interior of Iceland. The next 500 kilometers (311 miles) and five days would fall into a familiar rhythm. The daylight hours extend almost around the clock during the Icelandic summer, and the team made the most of the time, breaking camp early in order to minimize the number of river crossings they had to take. Often they would ride through dry river beds and along desiccated tracks on a constant look out for water that could be filtered and drank. The terrain would change subtly from day to day. A single gravel road →

was often barely distinguishable from the surface it passed through. At times it was slow and delicate riding, trying to avoid slashing a tire or catching a rear mech against a rock. At others the group hit sections of deep sand. Even with tire pressures dropped to nearly single figures, the riders were unable to find traction and had to resort to pushing for kilometers at a time. All the while they were whipped by wind and the finest of volcanic dust, which permeated every pore and small gap in clothing or luggage.

The evenings provided welcome respite, not just from the physical exertion, but from the sense of being alone in such a huge expanse of land. Small huts along the route offered more than shelter; they became a place to decompress, like a port in a sea of rock, dust, and ice. The interior of each hut would quickly be decorated with clothing hung to dry. The stove was in constant rotation making warm drinks and boiling water for dehydrated meals. Consuming enough calories was a constant battle. The sheer weight and bulk of food meant that the team was managing their own deficits and never quite replacing the calories they burned during the day. Incredibly, despite the hardships, there were

moments of luxury in this wildest of locations. Many of the huts had neighboring hot springs, offering the ultimate post-ride bath. Aching bodies would slip underwater, while the freezing air nipped at any exposed skin above the surface.

The quad saw barely any sign of life in the depths of the interior. It is hard to imagine a less hospitable place. Yet, the land itself seemed alive, whether it was the bubbling hot springs or the freeze-thaw cycle as rivers are born and die each day. Even the rock was alive. In general, we think of mountains being permanent, formed and eroded over millennia, barely changing in our lifetimes. But these landscapes evolve too. On their third day, the group rode past the Holuhraun lava field. Just a decade ago the second-largest lava →

TRAVERSING THE ELEMENTAL LAND-SCAPE WAS FULL OF CHALLENGES, FROM DEEP DUST TO GLACIAL MELTWATER RIVERS.

THERE ARE FEW PLACES
IN THE WORLD THAT
FEEL AS REMOTE AS THE
INTERIOR OF ICELAND.

ICELAND TRAVERSE

RIDING ACROSS THE INTERIOR OF THE COUNTRY FELT LIKE CHARTING A PATH ACROSS THE SEA. WHEN THEY FINALLY REACHED THE ACTUAL COAST, CIVILIZATION WAS WELCOME RELIEF.

field in Iceland did not exist. It was formed during a volcanic eruption in 2014.

On the sixth day, the team negotiated the roughest of terrain, a final crux before a 10 kilometer (6 mile) descent and the first signs they were leaving the interior behind. They met some Icelandic traffic in the form of horses and sheep, and hints of green returned to the visual palette.

The final section of the ride followed the coast of the Westfjords. Tarmac made for a welcome change, as did the prospect of resupplying at the first gas station they reached. With gummy candies restocked, the remaining three days of riding were a little more straightforward, but no less draining. The road undulated, occasionally turning inland and climbing away from the coast before descending back toward the sea. They picked wild blueberries from the side of the road as they traveled, passing ship and plane wrecks, before finally reaching Bjargtangar. There was no more land to cover after nearly 1,000 kilometers (621 miles) were behind them. In front of them, only the ocean. The first ever east-west self-supported cycling traverse of Iceland had been completed. ○

"THE LANDSCAPE OF ICELAND IS DEFINED BY CONTRASTS. THE HEART OF THE ISLAND FEELS A WORLD APART FROM THE RAGGED COAST LINE."

WESTFJORDS

NORTHWESTERN
REGION

AKUREYRI

FLÓKALUNDUR

MÝRARTUNGA

BJARGTANGAR

HVAMMSTANGI

LAUGAFELL

WESTERN
REGION

HVERAVELLIR

THINGVELLIR

REYKJAVIK

SELFOSS

VIK

N

NORTHEASTERN
REGION

EGILSSTADIR ◉

DALATANGI

ASKJA

LAUGARFELL

KISTUFELL

VATNAJOKULL
NATIONAL PARK

HÖFN

KEY TRIP NOTES

REGION/LOCATION(S):
East-west traverse of Iceland.
Starting at the most easterly
point, Dalatangi, and finishing at
the most westerly, Bjargtangar

CATEGORY:
Multiday, epic

DISTANCE:
971 km (603 mi), potentially longer
depending on how passable rivers are

TERRAIN:
Gravel tracks, deep sand, and volcanic rock

SKILL LEVEL:
Advanced. A highly committing route,
with limited to zero bail-out options.
Potential for extreme weather. The team
consulted with river guides, farmers,
and search and rescue, and recruited an
Icelandic production team to help build
the route to ensure safety and compliance
with environmental standards.

HIGHLIGHTS:
The unique landscape of Iceland's
interior and the sense of extreme
isolation and relaxing in a hot
spring after a hard day of riding.

ESSENTIAL GEAR/EQUIPMENT:
Warm clothing and sleep kit, camp and
survival gear, sufficient food, and other
supplies for seven to ten days of riding.

RESUPPLY INFO:
No resupply until you hit the road in
the Westfjords, which is over 600 km
(373 mi) into the route. Gas station
resupply options thereafter.

RIDE SEASON:
Summer

CONTRIBUTOR/RIDER INFO

Emily Batty, Adam Morka, Chris
Burkard, and Eric Batty completed the
traverse in August 2020. Emily is a two-
time Olympic mountain bike racer and
multiple Canadian national champion.
Her husband, Adam, is a former
professional racer. Chris Burkard
is a world-renowned professional
photographer. Eric Batty is an arborist
and adventure sports photographer.
He has completed and documented
multiple bike and ski expeditions.

BRUTAL BEAUTY: EXPERIENCING ISLANDS FROM THE SADDLE

→

ROUTE
ISLAND HOPPING

LOCATION
FAROE ISLANDS

THE FAROES ARE brutally honest, egalitarian even. Treating all visitors alike, the howling winds and piercing rain make no exceptions. The roads hug the most jagged and fractured coastlines before climbing up and over mountains with no summit, just clouds sitting on sweeping flanks.

It took only minutes for the threesome of Chris McClean, Fiola Foley, and Paul Errington to learn this lesson. They were soaked to the bone and frozen after a few kilometers of riding from the archipelago's airport on the island of Vágar. As they pedaled north to the spectacular waterfall at Múlafossur, rain soaked the sleeves of their waterproof jackets and road spray saturated their shorts in seconds. A torrent of water—in full flush given the climatic conditions—was free falling down to the sea far below. It was there that they learned their second lesson. The low, claustrophobic mist withdrew almost instantaneously. Just when you think the Faroes have you beat, they will give you something back and pull you in closer. The dark clouds over-head split for a second, allowing rays and shafts of light to pierce through. Patches of white gold danced on the turbulent sea's surface. The high ridges that form the natural bowl that drains into Múlafossur revealed them-selves, before the wind blew once again and drew closed the curtains of fog.

A trip to the Faroes can quite easily fall into a highlights reel. It is all too tempting to see it as a geological theme park full of breathtaking cliffs and sea stacks. Each corner in the road reveals another awesome (in the truest sense of the word) landscape. Traveling by bike gave the group a different perspective. They were able to take in the places in-between, locations and experiences that you will not find in a guidebook or shared on Instagram, but are no less moving than the must-see spots. While they rode, they felt like they were part of the islands and truly interacting with them, rather than just observing.

On the island of Eysturoy, the trio slogged up the steep switchback road on the side of Slættaratindur—the highest peak on the Faroes at 880 meters (2,887 feet)—and around to Eiði. There they visited Risin og Kellingin, or the "Giant and the Witch." The two sea stacks stand just off the coast, somehow both fragile and monolithic. Legend says the giants of →

Iceland decided that they wanted the Faroes for themselves. They dispatched the Giant and the Witch to the Faroe Islands to bring them back. They struggled through the night, but the islands stood firm and they could not move them. Like all creatures of the night, if the sun shone on a giant or witch, they would turn to stone. They were so preoccupied with their struggle, they did not notice time passing, and as dawn broke, a shaft of sunlight put a stop to their efforts by turning them to stone on the spot. They have stood there ever since, staring longingly across the ocean toward their home in Iceland, while fulmars and petrels plunge and glide around them.

It was hard not to feel some solidarity with Risin og Kellingin. There were times that riding on the Faroes felt as unforgiving a task as dragging them across the wild north Atlantic ocean. Yet, the islands had completely enchanted the riders. The foreboding weather had been balanced by welcoming locals. The very landscapes that made riding so challenging also made it so special. Even though the riders' time on the islands was coming to an end, they knew they were tied to this harsh but stunning archipelago. They would return again. ○

THERE WERE RARE MOMENTS WHEN THE SUN CAME OUT AND REVEALED THE FULL GLORY OF THE FAROES' LANDSCAPE AND TRADITIONAL ARCHITECTURE.

"THEY FELT LIKE THEY WERE PART OF THE ISLANDS AND TRULY INTERACTING WITH THEM, RATHER THAN JUST OBSERVING."

FOOTBALL WITH A VIEW: THE GROUP LINKED COASTAL COMMUNITIES AS THEY ISLAND-HOPPED THEIR WAY AROUND THE ARCHIPELAGO.

THERE WERE TIMES THAT RIDING ON THE FAROES FELT LIKE CIRCLING THE EDGE OF THE WORLD.

"JUST WHEN YOU THINK THE FAROES HAVE YOU BEAT, THEY WILL GIVE YOU SOMETHING BACK AND PULL YOU IN CLOSER."

KEY TRIP NOTES

REGION/LOCATION(S):
Crossing four of the
islands of the Faroes:
Eysturoy, Streymoy,
Vágar, and Suðuroy.

CATEGORY:
Island hopping tour

DISTANCE:
220 km (137 mi)

TERRAIN:
Mostly tarmac with a
few gravel and easy off-road
excursions. Many islands
are linked by tunnel. Not all
are permitted to be ridden
by bike.

SKILL LEVEL:
Intermediate. The weather
often makes even the mellowest
of roads a challenging
undertaking, and there are
plenty of steep climbs to
throw into the mix.

HIGHLIGHTS:
Experiencing the incredible
landscape, friendly locals,
and the culture of island life.

**ESSENTIAL GEAR/
EQUIPMENT:**
Waterproof layers and spare
warm gear. Be prepared for
any and all weather.

RESUPPLY INFO:
Most villages have small
supermarkets and gas
stations. Wild camping is not
legal. There are a number
of campsites on the islands,
but most are only open in the
summer months. Given the
potential for inclement weather,
you may prefer to book bed
and breakfasts and hotels.

RIDE SEASON:
Late April–late September

CONTRIBUTOR/RIDER INFO

Chris McClean is an award-
winning professional
photographer and filmmaker
specializing in surfing and
cycling. He traveled to the
Faroes with Fiola Foley and
Paul Errington.

INDEX

BIKEPACKING

→

Exploring the Roads Less Cycled

This book was conceived, edited, and designed by gestalten.
Edited by Robert Klanten, Andrea Servert
Contributing editor: Stefan Amato

Texts, maps, and illustrations by Stefan Amato
Journey texts by Tom Hill (pp.24–29, pp.40–59, pp.74–93, pp.100–103,
pp.110–117, pp. 148–155, pp.166–173, pp.180–189, pp.192–195,
pp.198–211, pp.216–257, pp.260–285)

Head of Design: Niklas Juli
Design, cover, and layout by Isabelle Emmerich
Photo Editor: Valentina Marinai

Typefaces: Montefiore, Minion Pro

Cover image by Jordan Gibbons
Backcover image by Chris McClean

Printed by Grafisches Centrum Cuno, Calbe (Saale)
Made in Germany

Published by gestalten, Berlin 2021
ISBN 978-3-96704-013-5

For more information, and to order books, please visit www.gestalten.com

Bibliographic information published by the Deutsche
Nationalbibliothek. The Deutsche Nationalbibliothek lists
this publication in the Deutsche Nationalbibliografie;
detailed bibliographic data is available online at www.dnb.de

This book was printed on paper certified according
to the standards of the FSC®.